This book was donated by:
Orville and Esther Beth Rogers
3840 West Bay Circle
Dallas, TX 75214-2925
In honor of the faithful service of Claude and
Jeannie Cone to NM Baptists for 20 years

THE MIRACLE YOU'VE BEEN SEARCHING FOR

THE MIRACLE YOU'VE BEEN SEARCHING FOR

MAC BRUNSON

MOODY PUBLISHERS
CHICAGO

All Scripture quotations, unless otherwise indicated, are taken from the *New American Standard Bible®*, Copyright © The Lockman Foundation 1960, 1962, 1963, 1968, 1971, 1972, 1973, 1975, 1977, 1995. Used by permission.

Scripture quotations marked NKJV are taken from the *New King James Version*. Copyright © 1982 by Thomas Nelson, Inc. Used by permission. All rights reserved.

Scripture quotations marked NIV are taken from the *Holy Bible, New International Version®*. NIV®. Copyright © 1973, 1978, 1984 by International Bible Society. Used by permission of Zondervan Publishing House. All rights reserved.

Scripture quotations marked KJV are taken from the King James Version.

Library of Congress Cataloging-in-Publication Data

Brunson, Mac, 1957-
 The miracle you've been searching for / Mac Brunson
     p. cm.
 ISBN 0-8024-1375-7
 1. Miracles. 2. Christian life—Baptist authors. I. Title
 BT97.3.B78 2004
 231.7'3—dc22

                              2004013866

              1 3 5 7 9 10 8 6 4 2
        Printed in the United States of America

To my dad, Donald McCall Brunson Sr.
who encouraged me to read the Word,
believe the Word,
love the Word
by his living the Word every day

CONTENTS

ACKNOWLEDGMENTS

ZACHARIAS PROPHESIES IN Luke 1:78: "Because of the tender mercy of our God, with which the Sunrise from on high will visit us . . . "

God is a God of great and tender mercies, and I have experienced that over and over again in my life. One of the ways I have experienced His tender mercies has been through those He has placed in my life and those He has directed across my path who have been like sunshine from on high.

Mark Tobey is my editor at Moody Publishing, and a real source of encouragement. Thank you Mark for believing in me enough to give me the opportunity to write. Tracy Sumner and Allan Sholes worked with the manuscript and offered invaluable insight and direction.

Sharron and George Kemp are my assistants and are such a daily blessing to me. Thank you for your godly character and your faithfulness, and for keeping me on target.

To the wonderful staff at First Baptist Church of Dallas. All of you play a major part in my ministry. You will never know how much I love you and am thankful that we are co-laborers together.

Jim Ward is the administrator of First Dallas and manages all the details so that I can concentrate on the main thing that God has called me to do.

I want to acknowledge some of God's greatest miracles in my life. Deb, your inspiration and faithful support have made much of my ministry possible. And Courtney, Trey, and Wills, you three are the miracles your mom and I were searching for!

INTRODUCTION: DOES GOD STILL MOVE?

DOES GOD STILL make miracles?

We live in a world where people need—sometimes desperately—God to move in their lives in a miraculous way. It's a world that needs to see the miraculous taking place in the church—in the lives of ordinary Christians like you and me.

In his book *Jesus Drives Me Crazy*, Leonard Sweet talks about the places where Christianity is growing. He states that Christianity is growing where there is: "belief in miracles and a personal God who cares enough to intervene directly in everyday life." He also points out where Christianity is in decline: "where faith is being passed on by churches for whom the Real Presence has vanished from the world, churches that no longer have confidence in the Scriptures or the Spirit, churches whose cold Christ can no longer warm the heart."[1]

But does God still "invade"? Sure, the Bible tells of three great "miracle periods" in the history of His redemption of His people: first, during the time of Moses and the Exodus; then during the ministry of the great prophets

Elijah and Elisha; and finally during the earthly ministry of Christ as recorded in the Gospels and in the age of the apostles as seen in the book of Acts. But now . . . ?

I believe that God still wants to do miracles in our lives, and I believe He wants to do that for two reasons: to bless us personally and to demonstrate to those around us that He is a God of power, a God who can get things done when no one or nothing else can.

There are any number of reasons people want to see miracles today. Some, like the people who followed Jesus daily during His earthly ministry, have real and pressing needs for a miracle. They need miracles in their home lives, in their financial situations, at work, or in their bodies.

Others treat miracles as a source of a "spiritual high," or as a means to keep their faith going. Like a man who is hopelessly addicted to an illicit drug and needs his "fix" to function physically and mentally, they need that miracle to function spiritually. If they don't get that miracle, they feel lost and lose what little faith they had.

Still others see miracles as a kind of spiritual entertainment. Near the end of Jesus' earthly ministry, King Herod had heard of Jesus and of the miracles He had performed out in the open for everyone to see. When the Jewish religious leaders brought Jesus before Herod, the king was glad to see him, simply because he wanted Him to do some kind of miracle for him to witness (see Luke 23:8).

But the Bible specifically tells us God's purpose for miracles. On the day of Pentecost, with the Holy Spirit coming down miraculously and spectacularly on that first group of believers, the apostle Peter told them, "Men of Israel, listen to these words: Jesus the Nazarene, a man attested to you by God with *miracles* and *wonders* and *signs* which God performed through Him in your midst . . ." (Acts 2:22, italics added). In other words, Jesus performed His miracles for the purpose of demonstrating to witnesses that He was indeed the Son of God, the long-awaited Messiah.

And I have some wonderful news concerning miracles: God does the same thing today!

In times of difficulty and despair and need, there is often no solution apart from a miracle of God. God's written Word, the Bible, teaches us that He is Lord even over life's limitations and stresses.

He is a God who still works miracles! That's what this book is all about.

I don't know what your situation is. Perhaps you're struggling with illness, or worried sick about money, or praying for your prodigal child to come home to Jesus—but you can't see how, humanly, any of this can happen. Whatever your need, I want you to see that the "age of miracles" is *not* over, that God still moves that way even today. I want you to see that Jesus wants to continue His miracle work in the lives of every one of us who are called by His name and who walk in faith and in obedience to His commands.

Are you in need, hurting, and looking for a miracle? Then read on!

Mac Brunson

1.   Leonard Sweet, *Jesus Drives Me Crazy* (Grand Rapids, Mich.: Zondervan Publishing House, 2003), 83.

CHAPTER ONE

JUST AS YOU ARE

It may well be that the world is denied miracle after miracle and triumph after triumph because we will not bring to Christ what we have and what we are.

■ WILLIAM BARCLAY

IS THE ECONOMY IMPROVING?

It depends on whom you ask. By some measures, yes. But if you ask one of the millions of Americans who have lost jobs in recent years—whether through being "downsized," having a high-tech job shipped overseas, or simply being fired—*their* economy isn't improving. Some of these jobless folks don't show up in the government's numbers —because they've stopped looking. They've given up.

It's an easy thing to do when you're in those straits. You pray, and you pray, and you search for the Lord's leading in His Word, and try to be obedient. But no job materializes. Meanwhile, money's getting tight. You feel as if you've done everything you can, yet your finances and even your faith are dwindling. You're running on empty, and where is God?

UP AGAINST OUR LIMITS

We've all been there. We've all been in a place of human limitations in the face of overwhelming needs. Our lives, our marriages, our families, our ministries all put more demands on us than our resources can cover. We don't quite know what to do.

Sometimes the demands we are called to meet put us in a place of discouragement, even resignation. We know there is no way we can meet our obligations, and we feel like giving up. Giving up on work—or even finding work. Giving up on our marriages and families. Giving up on church and ministry. Even giving up on God!

We know there is no way we can make the next house payment. No way we can cover the expenses of raising a family. No way we can accomplish the things God has called us to do. No way we can get through the trials we face. No way to realize our dreams of doing big things for the kingdom of God. We assess the needs placed before us, and we know we can't meet those needs. We are just too limited.

Limited in our financial resources.

Limited in our abilities.

Limited in our know-how.

Limited in our faith.

Even Jesus' disciples—the twelve men who traveled and ministered with Him daily, witnessing up close the miracles He performed—faced limitations when it came to doing what He had called them to do. Jesus knew that. He understood their humanity. But He never let a little thing like human limitations get in the way of accomplishing great things for the kingdom. In fact, He *used* their humanness, their limitations, to His glory, showing how God works through "clay pots," as Paul calls us. And He will begin with you *just as you are,* with what little you have . . . no matter how small.

In one miracle scene—one so profound and so spectacular that all four Gospel writers included it in their accounts of the life and work of Christ—Jesus showed the disciples how He could do great things with very little.

Remember how in the introduction we looked at the three great "miracle periods" in the Bible: the time of the Exodus, the era of Elijah and Elisha, and the earthly ministry of Jesus Himself, followed by the Acts of the Apostles. As we begin to look at the sixth chapter of Mark's gospel, Mark seems to be comparing and contrasting Moses and Christ. He describes the place by the sea as "lonely" and "desolate," evoking echoes of Moses leading the children of Israel through the wilderness. The Israelites became hungry in the wilderness, Moses prayed, and God sent manna from heaven.

Now, nearly 1,500 years later, here is Jesus with these Jews out in a deserted place, and again they're hungry. But this time Jesus Himself is the manna sent from heaven. In fact, in John 6:49–51, Jesus says that their fathers ate manna in the wilderness, but "I am the living bread that came down out of heaven; if any one eats of this bread, he will live forever . . ."

It was Elijah who told the widow in Zarephath

that the bowl of flour would not be exhausted nor the jar of oil emptied, but that she and her son would have bread (1 Kings 17:8–16). Here in Mark 6, the bread stretched much further than that.

It was Elisha who fed the one hundred prophets with twenty loaves of barley (see 2 Kings 4:42–44), but here again Jesus is going to feed multiplied thousands with five loaves and two fish. It seems that the text is telling us that here is One greater than the prophets!

In Mark 6:39, Jesus gives the command for the people to sit on the green grass. Your mind goes back to Psalm 23, where David writes that "the LORD is my shepherd . . . He makes me lie down in green pastures." Here is One who is greater than David. It is as if the Holy Spirit is pointing out that here is One who is greater than the law, the prophets, and the sacred writings. This sheds new light on Jesus' words: "Do not think that I came to abolish the Law or the Prophets; I did not come to abolish, but to fulfill" (Matthew 5:17–18). Here is the very Word of God in the flesh.

But while the disciples are busy in that lakeshore wilderness dividing all those people into groups and parceling out the barley loaves and fish, Herod is also hosting quite a different feast—a banquet at his palace.

You probably remember that Herod had taken his brother Philip's wife and eloped with her, even though they were both married. John the Baptist had confronted Herod, and the king was furious. Herod had the Baptist arrested, and, through the deception and manipulation of Salome, his stepdaughter, had John beheaded.

This shows us the contrasts between the two banquets. Herod's banquet was to pamper his ego and show off his power, but Jesus' banquet ministered to the needs of others. Herod's banquet had a political agenda, but Jesus' banquet had a kingdom agenda. Herod's banquet would end in death, but Jesus' banquet would give life.

"NOW WHAT?"

Of course, if you were one of the thousands who had followed Jesus to this remote spot, curious, hoping to hear Him speak or maybe even perform one of the miracles you had heard about, you never would have guessed He was going to host a feast! The scene was a large flat area at the foot of the hills surrounding the Sea of Galilee. It was a barren, dry area with little vegetation growing, just some large grassy areas probably stripped almost to bare soil by passing herds of sheep.

It was late in the day, close to sunset. Many of the people hadn't eaten since early that morning, and they were becoming very hungry. But before anyone said a word about feeding them, Jesus knew their needs. He looked out at the throng, and from the bottom of His heart He felt deep compassion for them.

He knew they needed direction and salvation, and He had a plan to meet those needs. But more immediately, they needed something to eat. He had a plan for meeting that need, too.

Still, He wasn't going to meet that need using the large amount of physical resources it would take to accomplish what needed to be done. Rather, His plan relied on the miraculous.

As nightfall approached, the disciples came to Jesus to tell Him that there were a lot of hungry people in the crowd and that it would be a good idea to send them away to the local villages so they could buy themselves something to eat. But Jesus had a different idea.

"*You* give them something to eat!" Jesus told the disciples. *The New Living Translation* shows the disciples' protest and confusion: "With what?" they asked. "It would take a small fortune to buy food for all this crowd!" (verse 37). In effect, they were arguing with the Master: "You want us to feed these people, but there is no way we can do it! We don't have any food, we don't have money to buy food, we're miles away from any supermarkets, and anyway, everything's closed. Now what?"

The disciples' reaction was much like that of a single parent who receives her son's $5,000 medical bill but who has barely enough money to put a roof over his head, food in his stomach, and clothes on his back. There is no medical insurance to fall back on and no foreseeable way she will come up with the cash to pay the bill. In a fit of frustration, anxiety and hopelessness, the mother tosses the bill aside, throws up her hands and exclaims to nobody in particular, "How am I going to pay for this?"

In John's account of this miracle scene, we read of

Philip, who assessed the financial situation. Jesus had just asked Philip where they could buy bread to feed all those people. Philip knew that the disciples among them couldn't come up with nearly enough money to pay for so much as a small meal for all these people, that it would take two-thirds of a year's salary to buy that much food. Even if they were near an open restaurant or grocery—and had a way of carting all that food back to the place by the lake—they didn't have enough money. Beyond that, it was getting late and they were feeling tired and frustrated. At that moment, the disciples were at the end of their rope.

HOW SOON WE FORGET

Here is the disciples' problem—a problem we can, perhaps, identify with. The disciples' problem at that moment wasn't just that they had no clue how they were going to take care of all those hungry people. Their problem was that they had forgotten *whom* they served and *what* He had already told them, taught them, and shown them.

Earlier, Jesus had given the disciples authority to cast out demonic spirits and to heal the sick and the lame. They were mere men, and Jesus was telling them they themselves would perform miracles in His name. He also gave them their marching orders: "Take nothing for their journey, except a mere staff—no bread, no bag, no money in their belt—but to wear sandals; and He added, 'Do not put on two tunics'" (Mark 6:8–9).

Jesus was telling them, in other words, "I am your source for everything you need. You needn't take anything with you, because I'm going to take care of everything."

The disciples obeyed Jesus' instructions to the letter, and they had done everything Jesus had said they would. They, everyday people like you and me, remember, preached with power, cast out demons, healed the sick—all of that after leaving their Lord and moving out in pairs. They had seen the power of Jesus Christ at work before their very eyes. They had seen people repent, seen demons flee in His name, and seen the sickest people restored to health.

But now, at the moment when Jesus was about to do something miraculous through them, they forgot what the power of God had already done through them. And they had taken their eyes off the fact that Jesus was right here with them.

Instead, they focused on their dwindling resources and lost opportunities. They didn't figure Jesus into the equation. Even after seeing the miracles Jesus had performed, even after performing those same kinds of miracles themselves, it never crossed their minds that Jesus was about to do something spectacular before their very eyes.

Jesus knew what was on the disciples' minds. He knew what was behind their questions. He knew that they not only doubted that they would feed the people; they believed with all their hearts and minds that it *couldn't* be done.

Now, Jesus had the disciples right where He wanted them!

LIMITED RESOURCES, LIMITLESS MIRACLES

Jesus didn't tell the disciples what He had in mind. He simply sent them out into the crowd to gather all the food they could find. Each of them went from person to person, telling them that the Master had asked them to give up whatever food they were carrying. Time after time, they came up empty. No one had anything to offer. These were, after all, hungry people, and they had probably already eaten whatever food they had carried with them for the day.

But one of the disciples, Andrew (Peter's brother), stumbled onto something. A small boy carrying all his belongings in a small sack volunteered that he had some food. The lad reached into the sack and pulled out five loaves of barley bread and two small fish he had packed for the day. Holding them up for the disciple, the boy cheerfully offered them up.

"Sir, this is all I have," he told Andrew apologetically, "It's not much, but if Jesus needs them He can have them."

When their search was complete, each of the disciples reported back to Jesus. Eleven of them came up empty. Only Andrew had found anything, and even he hadn't found much.

These were not loaves of bread and fish the way we think of them today. The loaves weren't the big slabs of wheat bread we in the West can buy in our grocery stores, and the fish weren't anything like the big Alaskan salmon we've seen. Far from it! In reality, the loaves were small, flat pieces of unleavened bread, probably about the size of small pancakes, and the fish were along the lines of small dried herring.

Now what do we do? the disciples must have been wondering. *How are we going to feed all these people with this little bit of food? Even the Teacher Himself can't make something out of nothing!*

The disciples saw an impossibility, yet Jesus saw not only a possibility, but a certainty that He could do great things with very little.

THE MIRACLE OF MUCH OUT OF LITTLE

"Go and have the people gather in groups of fifty to a hundred each and sit down on the grass," Jesus told the disciples.

The disciples still wondered just what Jesus had in mind. Yes, there was some food, but barely enough to feed a few people, let alone the thousands gathered that evening. Did He know about some source of food they didn't know about? Or was He just going to teach again, hoping the people would forget, if only for a short time, that they were hungry?

Five small loaves of bread and a couple of puny little fish, and He's asking us to have these people sit, as if we're going to feed them? the disciples must have been thinking. *What is He trying to do, start a riot?*

The disciples didn't understand what Jesus was doing, but they did as He had told them. In all their doubt, in all their frustration, they obeyed. Walking through the crowd, the disciples spread the word that Jesus had instructed people to gather in small groups and sit down in the grass and relax.

With the disciples and the crowd of thousands

looking on, Jesus took the bread and the fish, what little there was of both, and thanked His Father for His provision. Then He broke the loaves of bread and the fish and began giving them to the disciples to distribute to the crowd. We are told in Mark 6:41 that He blessed the food and broke the loaves and he *kept giving:* He broke and gave and broke and gave. The bread was multiplying in His hands.

He gave, and He continued giving. Then He gave some more. The more Jesus gave, the more He seemed to have to give.

Finally, when He was finished giving that evening, thousands of hungry people had had enough to eat. Not only that, but when the disciples had finished gathering the leftovers, twelve baskets *full* of food remained.

The disciples knew what they had just witnessed. This was not, as has been suggested in the centuries since this scene took place, a case of a crowd of thousands being moved to generosity by the willingness of one small boy to give what little he had. It wasn't a case of someone sneaking away to buy enough food to feed everyone there that night.

This was a miracle, plain and simple. None of the Twelve and none of the thousands there that evening could explain it or even fully understand it. After all, that's what a miracle is! It's God performing great things in the face of our limited knowledge, our limited skills, our limited resources.

They just knew they had witnessed something big coming from something very small.

THE LITTLE, THE LEAST, THE LAST?

In my hometown of Dallas, Texas, a mentality exists that everything has to be big. We like big houses, big cars, big salaries. People here seem to think that if something is small, then it can't be worth much. That's even true in the "Christian world" down here. We like big churches and big ministries down here. There seems to be the mentality that if it's small, then God can't be in it. But that is not just true only in Texas. All of us, no matter where we live, seem to be unimpressed with what we think is unimpressive: the little, the least, the last.

But the God we serve specializes in working with small things, in taking our human limitations and doing miracles.

The Old Testament prophet Zechariah wrote, "Do not despise these small beginnings . . ." (Zechariah 4:10, NLT). And the Bible shows us over and over that God loves to take little things and do great things with them. It was a small teenager with a small sling and a small rock who brought down a giant—a teenager who later became a great king of Israel. It was a little servant girl who took the mighty military leader Naaman to the prophet Elisha for cleansing from leprosy (see 2 Kings 5). And it was a little baby in a manger who was God in the flesh, who would one day teach and perform miracles the likes of which the world had never seen, who would give of Himself on a cross so that we could be reunited with our heavenly Father.

When you feel small, when you feel limited in your resources, you need to understand that our God is Lord of all, including the limitations life places on us. When you need a miracle in your life, you need to understand that God specializes in doing great things with very little.

Jesus gave the disciples clear instruction, *knowing* they didn't have the resources to follow them out. They protested and argued with Him. Even as they did as Jesus had instructed them, they rationalized and they doubted. They looked at what they had to offer and concluded that it couldn't be done.

So often, we're like those disciples. We have witnessed, maybe personally, what kinds of miracles He can perform. Time and time again, we have seen Him provide for us, and usually at just the right time. We have heard His powerful teaching. But when we get to where we desperately need a miracle, we lose our focus. We look not at our Provider and our source for everything we need, but at our limited, or nonexistent, resources.

When we take our focus off our Source, we can become anxious, frustrated, even panicky because we know we don't have "enough." We focus on our lost opportunities, at what we "should" have done before to solve our own problems and meet our own needs. Then, the hopelessness, that feeling of resignation, sets in. There is nothing we can do to help our situation.

That, friends, is when Jesus has us where He wants us. That is when we are in a place of total dependence on Him, a place where we have no choice but to focus on Him.

"I want you to depend on Me," the Lord tells us. "All you have to do is trust in Me and put what you have and what you are in My hands."

"But Lord, I don't have much to offer," we protest. "That's why I need a miracle in the first place."

"Then just place what you have in My hands, and watch what I can do," He answers.

I believe that at some point in our lives, God will put each of us in a place where we have no option but to trust in Him for a miracle. That may mean being in a place where we just don't believe we have the resources to do the things we need to do, in a place where we are physically, emotionally, and financially drained.

We all need to lay hold of the lesson Jesus intended in this miracle of feeding the thousands, and it's this: Our being in a place where we don't have the resources to do what He has called us to do does not prevent God from multiplying what we place in His hands.

We may not always understand why God has placed us in the situations we are in. Why we don't have the resources to do the things He has placed before us. Why we are in such dire need. Why nothing seems to be breaking right for us. Why things didn't turn out the way we had planned. *Why we need a miracle!*

But the truth is we don't always need to understand. Our lack of understanding—as well as our lack of resources—should never keep us from hearing God's Word and acting on it. When we do that, we learn the lesson Jesus laid out for the disciples on the shore of the Sea of Galilee. We learn that our lack of understanding and our lack of resources won't keep God from acting in a mighty and miraculous way.

We should always trust who we are and what we have to Jesus' hands. When we see limitations, He sees unlimited blessings. When we see impossibilities, He sees not just the possibilities but certainties of a blessing. When we see hopelessness, He sees miracles.

When you feel small and limited in your resources, then it's time to get your focus off yourself and what you don't have and on Jesus, who has everything you need. When you do that, you can rest assured that God will do with your limitations what He does so well.

It will be time for a miracle!

THE INCREDIBLE EXPANDING DOLLAR

There's a display case at Camp-of-the-Woods, a Christian resort and conference center located in the Adirondack Park of upstate New York. Inside is a single dollar bill. There's a story behind that dollar.

John H. Bechtel was a missionary to Hong Kong and a man with a dream. John longed to see Chinese children come to know Jesus Christ, and to that end, he had as his heart's desire opening a camp where he and others could work with and minister to these children. But there were questions to be answered before the camp could be opened, the first of which was *where* to build it.

Suddenly, John Bechtel's dream became a distinct possibility when the Christian Children's Fund, an organization dedicated to meeting the needs of children in all cultures and from all belief systems, decided to sell some of its property in Hong Kong. One day, representatives of the Christian Children's Fund approached him and asked if he wanted to purchase the property.

Did he ever! Bechtel told the people from the Christian Children's Fund of his plans and how the property they were offering to sell him would be perfect for what he believed God had led him to do. Yes, he told them, he wanted to buy it!

Bechtel believed this opportunity was the beginning of seeing his dream turn to reality. The Christian Children Fund's offer to sell him their property seemed to him a timely act of God, a small miracle.

That brought John Bechtel to the next hurdle on his way to opening his children's camp. He didn't have the money to purchase the property. But this man of faith wasn't going to let that stop him. He knew that if God wanted him to open the camp, He would make a way. The way Bechtel saw it, God had already provided the property; so it only made sense that He would provide the funds to buy it.

John Bechtel was a man of faith, but he was also a man of action. He believed God would provide the money he needed, but that it likely wouldn't happen if he didn't put some action behind his faith. He began writing and sending fund-raising letters and talking to as many people as he could, asking for donations so that he could buy the property and start his ministry.

Of course, Bechtel envisioned many thousands of dollars in donations rolling in once he had presented his plan. After all, who wouldn't want to be part of such a ministry?

But the donations didn't come. His requests for funding for the children's camp were met with almost total silence. Instead of receiving thousands of dollars in donations and pledges, he became part of what has to be one of the all-time greatest disappointments in Christian fund-raising history: He received just one dollar.

One little girl who had heard of John Bechtel's plan broke open her piggy bank and scraped together one dollar from her allowance money and sent it to Bechtel. But days, then weeks, then months passed without Bechtel receiving so much as another dime. A year after Bechtel had sent out his letters and began making his personal requests for funding, all he had in his ministry fund was the little girl's dollar bill.

John Bechtel was discouraged, even brokenhearted. He needed money to make his project happen, but he had none. He began to believe that his dream of starting a Christian ministry for children in China would be unrealized.

John Bechtel probably felt like giving up. But God wasn't finished with this man's dream. Not by a long shot.

Later, the Christian Children's Fund contacted Bechtel and asked him if he was still interested in purchasing the property. Of course he was still interested, but he had to tell the organization he had no funds to make the purchase. The Christian Children's Fund would have to find another buyer. And John Bechtel would have to wait and hope for another opportunity to begin his mission.

A short time after that conversation, however, the Christian Children's Fund came back to John Bechtel with another offer. They told him that God had led them to sell him the property and that they wanted him to have it.

The price? One American dollar.

I have never met John Bechtel in person, so I don't know exactly how he reacted to this incredible offer. But I can imagine his response was one of near-disbelief. I can imagine that his heart raced as he realized he— not to mention many children living in China—would be the beneficiary of a great miracle of God. And I can also imagine him calling everyone he knew, even those who couldn't afford to contribute to the cause, to tell them of the miracle he was watching unfold before his very eyes.

Not only had God provided the property on which John Bechtel would open his Christian camp, He had given him absolute confirmation that He was behind everything this missionary wanted to do.

Since John Bechtel purchased the property in 1971, more than 700,000 Chinese children, all of them raised in a culture that is almost exclusively Buddhist in religion, have come to what would be named the Suen Douh Camp to hear the gospel. Of those 700,000, more than 75,000 children have placed their faith in Jesus Christ.

This story is far more than the account of some magical coincidence. It's far more than some humanitarian organization looking to unload some property and, for all intents and purposes, *giving* it to a man with a dream. This account is an example of what God can do when we put whatever we have and whoever we are in His hands. One little girl gave all she had to John Bechtel's work, and as it turned out, it was just the right amount.

Maybe your dream isn't as expansive as a camp for children. Maybe your dream is simply to be able to afford new shoes or braces for your own kids, or to someday send your teenager to Christian college. Or to return to school yourself. Whatever you're longing for, even if it seems as far-off as the recent probe of Mars, God can make it happen, if you put what little you've got in His hands—and watch it multiply!

CONSIDER THIS

Do you think the evangelical church today buys into the bigger-is-better syndrome? What are some examples of this mentality? Can you think of any real-life examples of how God has used something seemingly small and insignificant?

DIGGING DEEPER

Explore the Bible for passages that focus both on "forgetting" and "remembering" what God has done.

STORM STORIES

The acid test of our faith in the promises of God is never found in the easygoing, comfortable ways of life, but in the great emergencies, the times of storm and of stress, the days of adversity, when all human aid fails.

■ ETHEL BELL

THERE'S A SHOW ON the Weather Channel called *Storm Stories*. It vividly and dramatically recounts, often through the tales of eyewitnesses, the stories of such disastrous storms as the great flood that swept the Netherlands in 1953, a tornado that struck an Illinois school in 1967, blizzards that buried Boston . . . you get the idea. As horrifying as these accounts are, the show is compelling to watch. It reminds us that these weather nightmares come out of nowhere, and that we are all vulnerable before what the narration usually calls "the fury of Mother Nature."

That's the thing about storms: They catch us unawares, falling on the just and the unjust. A Caribbean hurricane, for example, destroys the seacoast retreats of the wealthy *and* the flimsy shacks of the poor. And you can't really prepare for them. Oh, you can board up your windows, have flashlights at the ready in case of a power failure, head for the basement when the tornado siren goes off. But that won't stop the storm from striking.

"Life storms" can be like that, hitting us without much warning. Many of us, for example, have known someone whose spouse of many years confessed that he was having an affair and wanted out of the marriage —or maybe we've been there ourselves. That's a storm that appears to blow up out of nowhere and hit us broadside. Or the new management of our company comes in and hands pink slips to hundreds of loyal employees, and suddenly we're out of work. Or our mother is diagnosed as being in the early stages of Alzheimer's disease.

The tempest rages. Where do we turn?

TWELVE MEN AND THE SEA

That's what the disciples were feeling in Mark 6— after they had watched the Master perform the miracle of feeding thousands of people out of so little. Mark tells us that while Jesus went away to pray, He sent the Twelve on ahead in a boat, bound for Bethsaida. But then a storm came up. Mark tells us the apostles were "rowing against the wind." They were in trouble, in the middle of the sea, and awaiting a miracle. Not just *any* miracle, but a lifesaving miracle.

The kind of miracle one who faces a potentially terminal cancer hopes for.

The kind of miracle one looking down the barrel of financial ruin prays for.

The kind of miracle one watching his family fall apart before his very eyes begs for.

Looking at biblical events from our vantage point, we can forget that these were real guys, people like you and me. People to whom miracles don't happen. So I doubt that the apostles truly expected a miracle that night any more than many of us expect a miracle during our own times of crisis. All they knew was that they were in the middle of the Sea of Galilee, a body of water with a reputation for mischief, and they were in trouble.

Many of the Twelve probably knew at least one unfortunate fisherman who had met his end while trying to make his way back to the shore during one of this sea's legendary storms. Some of these men probably thought of the hapless souls lost in this sea during their own lifetimes. And they must have wondered if they were next.

The Sea of Galilee isn't large, but it boasts a well-deserved reputation for volatility. It lies in a depression surrounded by high mountains, making it an easy mark for windstorms. Around sunset during certain times of the year, cool, strong winds rise over the Mediterranean Sea and blow inland over the mountains that surround the sea, causing sudden and sometimes fierce storms.

Jesus' disciples, most of them fishermen or other kinds of "blue collar" workers, didn't understand the topographical factors that made the Sea of Galilee so dangerous. They just knew that they weren't making much progress. As hard as they rowed, the strong gusts of wind they were rowing against wiped out what little headway they made. It was an exhausting endeavor just to hold their position on the water.

Some of these men were hardly amateurs when it came to sailing in rough waters. At least four of them were experienced fishermen—men who for many years had made their living fishing on this very body of water, men who had been caught in storms before. They knew the Sea of Galilee like the back of their hand, and they knew how to handle a boat in rough water.

But now, they were caught in a storm and being blown around by the strong wind. Their muscles were in agony, their lungs ached for lack of oxygen, and their faces stung from the wind-driven droplets of seawater hitting their skin. Even worse, it was a stormy night, so they couldn't see where they were going.

These twelve men had to wonder why the Master sent them out there. Why, after a day of watching Him perform miracles and listening to His teaching, had He instructed them to sail—and why at the most dangerous part of the day? Most important, they had to wonder if He was going to do anything to save them now.

As you read this account in Mark 6, you cannot escape two things that are critical to the situation these men were in. First, Jesus put them in the boat and sent them out to sea *knowing* that they would encounter a storm. Second, Jesus was not with them. He sent them out by themselves and then went off to the mountain to pray.

Most of us have been in places in our lives where we understood all too well how the disciples must have felt. Stuck in the middle of what I'll call a "life storm," we wonder why God has sent us there, why He hasn't yet rescued us, and if He even *intends* to rescue us. During these life storms, we know we need a miracle and we need it now. But the question we often ask ourselves is this: Will God move in a miraculous way in *my* circumstances?

I will try to provide an answer to that question in the coming chapters. But before I do that, I want to give you something of a refresher course on stormy weather—the meteorological version.

STORM STATISTICS

We don't always know how or where storms will strike. But here are a few things weather and climate experts do know:

Storms are inevitable.

It is inevitable that Oklahoma will see tornadoes in April, that Buffalo will get snow in January, that parts of India will be drenched by monsoons at certain times of the year. Come August or thereabouts islanders in the Caribbean begin watching for hurricanes. We saw during the war in Iraq what damage sandstorms can do. People who live in Chicago know that in July, it isn't a question of whether it will thunderstorm, but when and how bad.

Life storms are like that too, as the apostle James pointed out in his epistle: "Consider it all joy . . . *when* you encounter various trials . . ." (James 1:2, italics added). This tells us that trials—family difficulties,

physical maladies, emotional upheavals, broken relationships, financial problems . . . *storms*—will be a
part of this journey we call our walk with Christ.

Storms are unpredictable.

On April 5, 1972, a class F3 tornado, one with
winds clocked from 158 to 206 miles per hour, struck
the quiet Pacific Northwest town of Vancouver, Washington, killing six people and injuring three hundred.
The storm destroyed or damaged homes, businesses,
and an elementary school. That year, the state of
Washington—not Texas, not Kansas, not Ohio, and
not Nebraska, all states known for tornadoes—led
the nation in tornado deaths.

In some parts of the country, six deaths due to a
tornado, while it would be seen as tragic, wouldn't
be terribly shocking. My home state of Texas, for
example, leads the nation in tornado occurrences
each year. But in Vancouver, which is located directly
across the Columbia River from Portland, Oregon,
no one expects to see a storm of this kind. Tornadoes
are rare in that area of the country, and tornadoes
that do the kind of damage this tornado did are practically unheard of.

This event was a tragic example of the unpre-
dictability of storms. While the people of Vancouver,
Washington knew that April 5, 1972 was likely going
to be a windy, rainy day—something the people in
the Pacific Northwest are well used to—they had no
idea that kind of devastation would befall their com-
munity that day.

The "life storms" we endure are very often like the one that hit Vancouver that spring afternoon. Life storms can arise in unexpected fashion and at any time, leaving us devastated and in need of a miracle. We may have no clue they are coming, and even if we do, we may have no idea how severe it will be.

We can't always accurately predict what life storms will head our way, and we need to be very careful when we try.

Storms don't care whom they hurt.

Maybe the scariest thing about natural storms is that they aren't "respecters of persons." By that I mean that a storm doesn't care if you are rich or poor, a celebrity or an unknown, a high-school dropout or a Ph.D., or whether you are driving a 1973 Pinto or a Cadillac Escalade. When a storm blows into an area, if you are too slow to get out of its path, you can get hurt, no matter who you are, what you know, or what you own.

The storms of life are the same way. They are often arbitrary, capricious, and cruel, not caring whom they harm or how badly. These storms blow into everybody's lives, regardless of social standing, academic achievement, or the size of your stock-market portfolio.

As children of God, we also need to understand that having a personal relationship with the living God doesn't guarantee sunny, San Diego-style weather year-round. Sometimes our lives are going to feel like they're being buffeted by a Category 5 hurricane similar to deadly Andrew that ravaged south Florida some years back. We may be wonderful, godly people—but, living in a fallen world, we'll see the darkness descend.

THROUGH NO FAULT OF OUR OWN

Linda (name changed) was a teacher, wife, mother of three, alto in her church choir, active in women's ministries. When she was not yet forty, Linda was diagnosed with breast cancer. At a women's retreat her friends gathered around her and prayed and cried and laid hands on her as she was about to undergo a course of chemotherapy. The initial treatments were effective, and she reached her five-year mark. She resumed her life, raised her kids, went back to work. Eventually, though, the cancer returned, and gentle Linda went to live with Jesus forever.

What did Linda do to "cause" her cancer?

Nothing.

These are some of the hardest life storms to face, the ones that blindside us. It's the non-drinking, honor-student teenager who's driving the speed limit and is struck by a drunken driver. It's the small businessman whose livelihood is swept away by global market forces beyond his control. It's the grandmother whose mind is slowly being blotted out by the fog of Alzheimer's disease.

These we might call "storms of circumstance." They attack simply because of the world we live in, a world where disease and death and disaster stalk the just and the unjust alike. Only when we enter fully into God's eternal kingdom will we be free of the effects of these kinds of storms. In fact, King Solomon, one of the wisest men who ever lived, suggested that storms of circumstance are just a fact of life, that there is no way we can completely avoid them: "*When* your dread comes like a storm and your calamity comes on like a whirlwind, *when* distress and anguish come upon you" (Proverbs 1:27, italics added).

Because we, too, are fallen as human beings, we can be selfish, immature, angry, fearful . . . or just plain stupid. "Relational storms" are among the most painful and problematic trials we can face, as anyone can attest who has gone through a divorce, a quarrel with an adult sibling, an estrangement with a grown child—or just has to deal with a difficult and demanding boss everyday.

We also must endure what I call "vocational storms." Will I be fired? Why was I fired? Why can't I find a job that suits my gifts? Does no one want me? I don't want to be here in this office, but how can I leave when my family needs the benefits? These questions can cut to the very core of our sense of self-worth. We can hear over and over that our identity is in Christ, and it is, but when we've been rejected yet again, it's hard to hold those truths in our heart.

All of these storms can play havoc with our emotions—which creates its own storm. First there's the event; then there's our *response* to the event. Sometimes an emotional storm can assail us out of the blue.

For the follower of Christ, "emotional storms" can be the most difficult to endure. We know that God says

"Trust me," but we struggle in our faith. We know that God says "Be at peace," but inside we are in turmoil, wondering what is next for us. We know that God says "Fear not," but we can feel the fear gnawing at our guts. And we think, *It's not supposed to be this way!*

BRINGERS OF BAD WEATHER

Then there are those times we can point to the *who* and the *why* of life storms. Let's start with the most obvious enemy:

Satan.

Many people of faith are under the impression— and a false one it is—that Satan has no power to touch us, that there is nothing he can do to bring storms into our lives. But the story of one very well-known Bible character shows otherwise.

Job was a godly man and well respected too. That made him a target of the attacks of Satan, the great accuser who went before God and issued this challenge: "If you let me send some tests Job's way, I know he'd curse Your name."

So God, knowing what kind of man Job was, gave the devil permission to send some horrendous life storms his way. First, all of his livestock—a measure of wealth and prosperity in those days—were stolen or killed. Then a powerful storm arose out of nowhere and killed all of Job's children.

Job grieved over his loss, but he still praised God. In the midst of all he had to endure, not one sinful word escaped his mouth, and not one thought of blame toward his Lord entered his mind.

But Satan wasn't finished. He was sure that if he just sent more storms Job's way, he could get him to curse God. So the devil appeared before God again and issued another challenge: "OK, so Job didn't turn his back on you when I took his possessions and his children. But if you let me take away his health, I know he'd curse You for it!"

God gave the devil permission to afflict Job's body, but with one condition: He would not be allowed to take Job's life. So Satan did as he was allowed to do, touching Job's body and causing it to be covered with huge, painful, running sores.

There Job was, all his children dead, all his wealth but a memory, and suffering horrible agony. All he had to turn to was his wife and his friends, none of whom offered him any *real* comfort. In effect, Job was alone in his suffering. Alone but for the continued fellowship with his God.

One life storm is bad enough for a man of God like Job to endure, but he had to endure a series of horrific storms. While Job had a lot of questions for the Lord, he still never cursed Him or turned away from Him. In the end, God performed a miracle in the midst of Job's life storms. Job kept his relationship with God intact, and the Lord restored Job to his former greatness.

When we are going through a life storm and looking for a miracle, we need to understand that there is a real-life Satan and that he hates us with a passion and will do anything he can to destroy us or at least

hurt us as badly as he can. And we need to understand that while God keeps the devil on a short leash
and that his eternal destination has already been
determined, he has limited power to bring storms
into our lives.

We also need to understand that when we are living godly lives, when we are seeking out and doing the
Lord's will, when we are doing those things that bring us
into closer fellowship with Him, we are sure to encounter
opposition, both from this world and from the one
who has been given a degree of dominion over it.

In his book *Lessons From a Life Coach*, Crawford W.
Loritts Jr., recalls something a Vietnam fighter pilot
told him about flying missions in a war: "You know
you're flying over the right target when you're being
shot at."[1]

Our life in Christ is like that. When we are "flying
over the right target," it gets the enemy's attention.
He'll do everything he can within his power to send
storms our way and get us off course and away from
the goals and targets God has put before us.

I believe this is one of the reasons we can, as James
put it, "Consider it all joy when [we] encounter various trials" (James 1:2). James went on to say that the
trials help us in the perfecting and maturing of our
faith. True enough! But it is equally true that we can
rejoice in some of our life storms, knowing that they
are often proof we are doing something right.

Our own stubbornness.

Some of our life storms come as a result of our

own stubbornness and hardheadedness. The New Testament contains an account of how the stubbornness of men led to a near-disaster off the coast of the island nation of Malta.

Luke, the physician, recorded in the twenty-seventh chapter of Acts how a ship—containing its cargo, the crew, and some prisoners, including the apostle Paul, who had an appointment with Caesar—set sail for Crete. The authorities on the ship had made journeys like this one many times, and they believed that as long as they took the right route, this would be another routine trip.

But Paul knew something was wrong. He had already survived a couple of storms himself, and he knew that it was getting late in the year to be starting a voyage like this.

"Look, fellas, this is not a good idea," the apostle told them. "If we set sail now, there's going to be trouble."

Paul was to be a prisoner in transit on the ship, but the crew knew there was something very real about this man and his God. Still, they didn't pay heed to his warnings. Instead, they stubbornly plowed ahead with their plans to set sail for Crete. Julius, the Roman centurion and the man who had the authority on the ship, took the word of the captain and the ship's crew, who told him the trip would be safe.

So they set sail, traveling westward along the south side of Crete to avoid the strong northeast winds. But before long, the ship was met by a storm—the *euraquilo*, strong winds that often blew through the west and central

Mediterranean. What had been a moderate wind, just right for sailing, became a violent storm, and the ship was blown dangerously off course.

Luke recorded in some detail how the ship was tossed around on the sea by the violent winds, then spun out of control and began breaking up. The ship was in danger of running aground in the shallows, so the crew started throwing cargo and tackle overboard to lighten the load. Even worse, the storm clouds kept the sun and stars covered for days on end, and the sailors had no idea what direction they were headed (verse 20).

There they were, lost at sea with a powerful storm tearing the ship apart. Luke recorded how the crew and passengers had resigned themselves to dying in a shipwreck: "from then on all hope of our being saved was gradually abandoned." Just off the shore of the island nation of Malta, the ship finally came apart, and only through a miracle of God were the men on the ship saved.

All of that because of a few men's stubbornness. Had the centurion heeded Paul's warning and stayed in port for a time, the ship and its passengers would have avoided the violent storm that cost them the ship and its contents and almost their lives.

The same applies to us when it comes to heeding the warnings God sends our way through His Word, through His promptings, and through the wise counsel of others. But so often we want to do what *we* want to do, regardless of who else is affected or what we know in our hearts to be God's desire for us. Like the foolish crew on Paul's ship, we think nothing is going to go wrong if we head in the wrong direction, pursuing the wrong job, the wrong relationship, the wrong course in life. We may not bring down a catastrophic storm on our heads; we may not get shipwrecked; but we can sure get ourselves in a lot of trouble . . . avoidable trouble.

Our own sin.

I once heard the story of a Christian man—we'll call him Phil—who had always done the "right things" in his Christian walk. He had been active in his church for years, had given generously to various Christian ministries, had read his Bible and prayed daily, and had even led some men's Bible studies.

One night, Phil "met" a woman over the Internet. He felt that he had a lot in common with this woman, and they really hit it off. It seemed that they could talk about anything. Their chats became phone calls; phone calls became in-person meetings (just for coffee at first), and in short order the personal meetings became an adulterous affair.

For several months, Phil kept his relationship with this "other woman" a secret, even from his very closest friends. Before long, though, Phil's life began to unravel. His business began to fail and his personal relationships—including those with his wife and children—suffered. Before long, he had to declare bankruptcy. A short time later, his wife took their children and left him.

Now, broke and alone, Phil confided in his best friend about what had been going on with the woman he had met only months before. The friend, heartsick at the man's fall into sin, gently and lovingly suggested that the storm that had raged in the man's life since the start of the adulterous relationship might be God's way of disciplining him for his sin.

Phil listened, but he wasn't buying it. "I just can't believe God would do this to me," he said. "I just don't believe He works that way."

Too many of us think like Phil. We can't believe that God would "work that way," allowing the storm to rage as a way of teaching us. But, as the Bible teaches, God does exactly that. Case in point: Jonah.

God had called Jonah to go to a big city called Nineveh and call its rebellious, sinful people to repentance. But there was a problem. Jonah didn't want to go. So instead of obeying the Lord, Jonah boarded a ship and headed for a place called Tarshish, where he thought he might find an escape from God's call to preach in Nineveh.

And where did Jonah's "escape" lead him? Right into the teeth of a horrendous storm, a storm so violent and so powerful that the ship was about to fall apart, sending its crew to a watery death.

The sailors, in a state of absolute panic, cried out to their gods then cast lots to find out who was responsible for bringing such a storm on them. As the Bible tells us, "the lot fell on Jonah" (Jonah 1:7). They confronted Jonah, who confessed to them that he was a prophet of God in rebellion and the reason everyone's life was in jeopardy.

"How could you do that to us?" they asked Jonah. "Now what should we do to calm this storm?"

"I'm the reason for this storm," Jonah answered, "So there's nothing you can do but throw me overboard. Do that, and the storm will end."

These terrified sailors took Jonah and tossed him overboard like a piece of unwanted cargo. Immediately the sea became calm. The ship and its crew were saved. Jonah, on the other hand, went from one storm to another, as he was swallowed by a giant sea creature. He spent the next three days in a place possibly so foul, smelly, and horrible that it defies human comprehension. In the midst of that unpleasantness, Jonah cried out to God for forgiveness and restoration.

This story had a happy ending. After that sea creature vomited the prophet onto the beach, Jonah (no doubt after taking at least a few minutes to get cleaned up a little) did as God had told him to do in the first place. He traveled to Nineveh and preached to the people, who turned away from their rebellion and turned back to God.

The beauty of this is that it is yet another demonstration of the love of God, who tells us in the midst of our self-induced life storms: "I love you so much and am so concerned with your life here on earth, that I would rather send you into the most terrible storm than see you drown in your own sin and rebelliousness."

The writer of the epistle to the Hebrews wrote of this Fatherly love, "For those whom the Lord loves He disciplines, and he scourges every son whom He receives. It is for discipline that you endure; God deals with you as with sons; for what son is there whom his father does not discipline?" (Hebrews 12:6–7).

The storms we endure because of our own rebellion are never pleasant. But, as the writer of Hebrews tell us, we can rejoice in them, for they are proof that God not only loves us enough to discipline us, but that He is there for us during the storms themselves.

We all have "storm stories" to tell—some more vivid and dramatic than others, but all testifying to the God who loves us enough to hold us through the rain and darkness and raging wind—until we come safely onto shore.

CONSIDER THIS

Reflect on times in your life when your response to a "storm" has eased it—or made it worse. What can you learn about how you deal with hard times?

DIGGING DEEPER

If you aren't very familiar with the "minor" prophets, like Jonah, read through several of the books—and see what they say about God's very personal dealings with His people.

1. Crawford W. Loritts Jr., *Lessons From a Life Coach* (Chicago: Moody Publishers, 2001).

OUR QUESTIONS, GOD'S ANSWERS

You will never find Jesus so precious as when the world is one vast howling wilderness. Then he is like a rose blooming in the midst of the desolation, a rock rising above the storm.

■ ROBERT MURRAY M'CHEYNE

IMAGINE BEING TOLD YOUR toddler might be growing old too fast.

That's what happened to my wife, Debbie, and me in 1988. Our 15-month-old son, Wills, had mysteriously stopped growing. We took him to a series of doctors, who could only speculate about a diagnosis. It might be cancer, they said, or a tumor. Or it might be something called Hutchinson-Gilford Progeria Syndrome, an extremely rare genetic disease that accelerates the aging process to about seven times the normal rate. We took our son to the Children's Medical Center at the University of Virginia Health Sciences Center, where he was treated by a world-renowned endocrinologist.

In what we considered a miracle of God, our son suddenly began growing again. The doctors never did find anything wrong. Since then, he has continued to live a normal life.

But that was far from the end of our health-related storms. Debbie's mother had passed away just before our scare with our son. She had suffered a long and painful dying from breast cancer, and Debbie was still grieving her loss when we found out that she could very well have the same illness that took her mother's life.

During a routine breast exam in March of 1990, Debbie's doctor discovered an abnormality called mammographic dysplasia, a condition that often precedes full-blown cancer. Knowing that Debbie's family had a history of breast cancer—in addition to her mother, six other women in her immediate family had succumbed to the disease—he scheduled her for immediate surgery.

IN THE WAITING ROOM

I remember as if it was yesterday the morning Debbie went in for her surgery. I could see the uneasiness and apprehension in her eyes. I knew she was thinking about those seven lost women in her family, and I knew she was wondering if she would be next.

I was thinking the same thing myself.

"Will you be there when I wake up?" Debbie asked me over and over as she prepared herself for the surgery. It was all I could do—be there—and it was all she wanted.

That morning, just minutes before Debbie was taken in for surgery, I led us in prayer. Debbie and I clung to our faith in Jesus Christ like shipwreck victims clinging to a life vest.

At around six o'clock that March morning, Debbie went in for a bilateral mastectomy.

With Debbie in surgery, I sat alone in the waiting room, which was deserted. No doctors strode through on morning rounds; no nurses bustled by. Not so much as a hospital volunteer pushing a flower cart came through the area. No family, no friends shared my vigil. I was alone, helpless, and angry.

There were so many as-yet unanswered questions. What would follow the surgery? Would my wife develop full-blown breast cancer? Would she have to undergo the torturous chemotherapy treatments many cancer patients must endure if they are to survive? *Would* she survive, long term?

I had a nightmarish sense of our life together unraveling right in front of us. I knew there was a very real chance that she could die—and that was a thought I could not bear.

We had gone through so much. I was pastoring in a difficult area of the city, and Deb's mother had died a very long and painful death. We had gone through ten months of agony, not knowing what was wrong with Wills, not knowing if he would live a normal life or if he would survive at all. Now this. She was only 33.

I wanted to know *"Why?"*

How could this be happening to us? I wondered. *How could God have allowed my wonderful, beautiful wife to be stricken this way? Why, when we had already gone through*

*the ordeal with Wills and the death of Debbie's dear mother,
did we have to go through more fear and suffering? Lord,
where are You in all of this?*

I begged and pleaded with God for a miracle, all
the while asking Him "Why?" I was about to receive an
answer.

WHY, LORD?

"Everything happens for a reason." We've all heard
that little nugget of "wisdom," offered up by well-
meaning friends who see us suffering through a life
storm and needing a miracle. They mean to help, but
it doesn't help and it doesn't comfort. *Reason? For this
kind of suffering?* Well, maybe.

First, though, let's return to the Sea of Galilee one
very stormy night.

Jesus gave a very firm command that the disciples
get in the boat and sail (see Mark 6:45). He had just
finished the miracle of the feeding of the 5,000 when
He gave them their orders. After hearing His teaching
and seeing Him perform miracles among the people,
the disciples were probably in no mood to head out to
sea and leave Him behind.

Jesus didn't just send the disciples out to toy with
them or to show them who was in charge. No, He had
a plan, and that plan was to teach the disciples something about Himself and to move their faith to a
newer, higher plane. In order to do that, He wanted
them in the boat.

It was early and dark outside when the disciples
boarded their boat and set out on their journey to

OUR QUESTIONS, GOD'S ANSWERS

Capernaum. John tells us that they had rowed only about three or four miles (John 6:19) in heavy wind and rough water. From where they were, it was a relatively easy trip that should not have taken an hour. But they had been in the boat for only a short period of time when the storm blew in and pushed them out to sea.

Amazingly, this was not the first time the disciples were caught in a storm in the Sea of Galilee. Two chapters earlier, Mark records how the disciples were in the same Sea of Galilee—probably in the very same boat—when what was likely a much more severe storm came upon them.

As He would do after the feeding of the 5,000, Jesus commanded the disciples to get in the boat and cross to the other side of the sea. On this occasion, however, He was going to be traveling with them.

The disciples filed into the boat and took their seats. Jesus joined them and took a comfortable spot in the stern where He could lay His head on a cushion and catch a nap during the trip. One could imagine that as the boat moved away from the shore, the disciples passed the time telling stories and talking about the day's events as they rowed. Jesus, meanwhile, was sound asleep. Yes, Jesus was fully God in the flesh, but He had also willingly become fully human, and He probably needed rest after a long day of teaching and preaching.

Then, one of those sudden Sea of Galilee storms blew in over the lake. It was a bad one, too. The wind-whipped waves crashed all around the disciples' boat

—and *into* the boat, tossing it around like a bath toy in the hands of an overly playful child.

These twelve men looked at what was going on around them and descended into a state of panic. I can imagine them screaming in fear, some vomiting from seasickness, some just cringing in the bottom of the boat waiting for what appeared to be certain death. At that moment, it seemed to them that there was nothing they could do to get themselves through this night.

Through it all, God in the flesh lay peacefully asleep in the stern, the back of the boat, seemingly unaware of what was going on around Him. Finally, when they were out of options, the disciples screamed to their Master: "Wake up! Don't you care that we're all going to die? Save us *and* Yourself!"

Immediately, Jesus awoke from His sound sleep, surveyed the situation, then took action. No, He didn't jump up and grab one of the oars to help hold the boat steady. He didn't start helping these terrified disciples bale the water out of their swamped vessel. He didn't bark out orders to the confused, frightened disciples.

He just spoke.

"Hush!" He said in a calm voice, speaking not to His panicked disciples but to the sea itself. "Be still!" and in an instant the wind and the waves died down. All was calm.

The disciples, soaked and shivering, were wide-eyed with fear and wonder. This man had proved Himself not only a wonderful teacher, like none any of them had ever heard, but one who with only three words could put a stop to a violent storm.

"Who is this? Even the wind and the waves obey him!" they said, wondering among themselves (see Mark 4:41).

Hush! Be still! Now, just days later, they were again in a boat, again in a storm. But there was one big difference. This time, Jesus was nowhere to be seen.

WHEN WE *NEED* A STORM

As they struggled just to keep the boat on course, the disciples' minds probably didn't turn to the miracle Jesus had performed on that very same boat before. All they knew was that He had seemingly sent them out to the middle of that sea at night to face a storm and left them alone to fend for themselves and maybe to die.

I think a lot of us can identify with how the disciples felt that night. It's so easy to remember the times when we needed a miracle and Jesus was right there for us. But what about those times when things move past needy to desperate and from desperate to hopeless? What about those times when, no matter how hard we look, we just can't seem to see Jesus in the midst of our storm?

Who among us haven't at some point looked at what appeared to be a hopeless situation, pounded our fists on our desks or bed, and asked out loud, "God, are you going to let me drown? Please wake up! Please help me!" and heard only silence? Who among us, when we were faced with financial catastrophe, family breakdown, or other life storms haven't wondered if God was even aware of what was going on? Who among us haven't been in a place in our lives of echoing the psalmist, who in one of these times of perceived isolation cried out, "Awake, O Lord! Why do you sleep? Rouse yourself!" (Psalm 44:23 NIV).

During the times we must endure life storms, the devil loves nothing more than to have us believe that we are alone, that God, our church, our friends, and our family have all abandoned us.

But as children of God, we can know positively that we are never alone.

God has promised us repeatedly that He's not going anywhere, that He is with us during times of calm and during times of storm. Following His death and resurrection, Jesus promised the disciples, "Surely I am with you *always*, to the very end of the age" (Matthew 28:20, NIV, italics added). Later, the writer of Hebrews recorded these words from the Lord: "Never will I leave you; never will I forsake you" (Hebrews 13:5 NIV).

God's love is one of devotion unending and immeasurable. When we belong to Him, He will never turn His back on us, never stop loving us, never leave us to fend for ourselves. I'll talk about that more in the next chapter. But for now, I want you to understand that God's love is also the kind of love that will do anything it takes to bring about the growth and maturity of our faith.

That includes allowing some storms to come our way. He did that twice for the disciples, and He'll certainly do it for us.

A lot of believers have a hard time swallowing that. "God would never send one of His own out to face a storm like that!" they protest. "That's just not like Him!"

The problem with that kind of thinking is this: If we believe that Jesus Christ was fully God—and if we belong to Him, we *do* believe that—then we have no option but to believe that He knew about the storms the disciples would have to endure *before* He sent them out to sea. Taking that a step further, when we are in the midst of life storms ourselves, we have no option but to believe that God knows what we are going to go through *before* it happens.

"But why?" you may be asking. "Why would a loving God send me into this life storm knowing how much I would suffer? Why would He put me in a place in life where I would have to endure such anguish and fear?"

If you are now in the midst of a life storm and looking for a miracle, you need to understand some things about God, about His love, and about His methods of protecting us, correcting us, and shaping us so that we can become more mature in our faith—become more like Him. You need to understand that His protection, correction, and shaping of us often includes putting us through some life storms. And you need to understand that as followers of Christ, we can know that the storms we go through are the very kinds of storms God wants to use to accomplish those goals.

When we are in the midst of a life storm—the loss

of a job, a hurtful breakup, a serious illness, or the death of a loved one—the natural reaction is to ask "Why?" or to complain and become bitter, maybe at God Himself. After all, we think, *if God controls everything, then why couldn't He stop this terrible thing from happening to me?*

That seems such a valid question for someone who is going through a life storm and needing a miracle. But when we have a real relationship with the God of the universe through His Son Jesus Christ, we don't have to look at life storms only in terms of our discomfort or suffering. Rather, we can look at them and rest assured in the truth that God has a purpose for what we are enduring, that He is doing something good in our lives through these storms.

As the apostle Paul wrote to the first-century church in Rome, a group of believers who were personally familiar with life storms, "And we know that God *causes all* things to work together for good to those who love God, to those who are called according to His purpose" (Romans 8:28, italics added). We who are called to be children of God can be assured that truly *everything* happens for a reason.

Just ask Larry Walker—or John Wesley.

THE SICKNESS THAT SAVED A LIFE

Larry Walker is a friend of mine and of many others in our church. He's been in ministry for decades and has traveled all over the world to take the gospel to places such as India, Africa, and South America, just to name a few.

Recently, Larry became very sick. His illness had become a chronic problem, and eventually he had become so sick that he had to be admitted to a local hospital. The problem? For some time, Larry and his doctors believed that during one of his mission trips he had ingested some kind of illness-causing parasite.

But the problem turned out far more serious than Larry or his doctors originally believed. During one of Larry's many physical examinations, his doctor discovered that he had a severe heart problem: an ailing aortic valve, which made him a candidate for massive heart failure. Almost immediately, Larry was scheduled for quadruple bypass surgery, a surgery I am happy to report was successful.

There is a great irony in all of this: The misery and sickness Larry endured for so long turned out to be the very thing that saved his life. Had he not become so sick, and had his doctors not believed that he had ingested a parasite, it's very possible that his heart could have given out without warning and he could have died.

Struggling with a chronic sickness you think is due to the invasion of some sort of bug certainly qualifies as a "life storm." But God used that particular storm to keep him from one that would have been far worse. He used it to save his life.

I believe that was one of the reasons Jesus sent His disciples into the midst of the storm recorded in Mark 6. Jesus had just performed His best-known miracle: the feeding of more than 5,000 people, using nothing more than five loaves of bread and a couple of little fish. As the disciples and the thousands of others at the scene basked in the afterglow of witnessing such a powerful miracle, Jesus sent the Twelve out to sea. But why would He send them away when they should have stayed on shore and celebrated? Why not just have them stay with the people and continue ministering as they had before?

There was one very good reason for Jesus to send the Twelve away that night.

This 5,000-man (and who knows how many women and children) throng had begun following Jesus because they believed He was there to lead the nation of Israel back to its past greatness. The Jews, influenced by the religious and political leaders of the time, had long looked for a military-type messiah, a man who would lead them in revolt against Roman rule and oppression and restore Israel to her former glory.

Jesus had just fed these men, and now they were ready to practically force Him to be their king and military leader (John 6:15). This multitude wasn't about to *ask* Jesus His permission to be this kind of leader. In this verse, we read that they intended to take Him by force. The word in the original language means *violence.* These men looked around them, and they knew that there were about 5,000 of them there that day—the same number of men in a Roman legion. They saw Jesus as another great military leader of their nation—along the lines of David and Joshua—and they were ready to move *right now.*

Jesus had called the twelve disciples to be His very

own apostles, but He knew it was part of their human nature to want and enjoy power. He also realized that the disciples could very likely have gotten caught up in the "power grab" and gotten whipped into a frenzy with the rest of the crowd. He sent them away so He could disperse the crowd Himself. Jesus knew that if His disciples got caught up in the militant fervor of the crowd, it could have ruined them for what He had planned for them to achieve in His name. By sending the Twelve into the storm over the Sea of Galilee, He allowed them to remain part of His plan.

The same is often true for us. I believe that when we are in the midst of even the worst life storms, our reaction as children of the King should be to thank God, for it may be that He allowed the very trauma we're going through at the moment for the purpose of preventing us from going through storms that might well destroy us or hinder us in doing what He has called us to do.

That, friends, is a miracle in and of itself!

"THE MOST GLORIOUS DAY"

John Wesley, one of the most influential and important preachers in the history of Christianity, once endured a literal storm that changed his life.

On October 17, 1735, John and his brother Charles boarded the *Simmonds*, a 220-ton vessel, for one of their many trans-Atlantic voyages. Twenty-six Moravians, members of a German Protestant group, as well as eighty English colonists accompanied the Wesleys on the trip.

On November 23, the *Simmonds* sailed into a horrendous storm, a storm so violent and powerful that it snapped the ship's main mast and shredded her mainsail. The waves broke over the sides of the ship with a noise Wesley later said "I could compare to nothing but large cannon or American thunder." The wind was so fierce and the waves so ferocious that the helmsman had no choice but to let the wind take the *Simmonds* where it would.

Wesley wrote of the incident in his journal: "Now, indeed, we could say, 'the waves of the sea were mighty, and raged horribly.' They rose up to the heavens above, and 'clave down to hell beneath.' The winds roared round about us. . . . The ship not only rocked to and fro with the utmost violence, but shook and jarred with so unequal, grating a motion, that one could not but with great difficulty keep one's hold of anything, nor stand a moment without it. Every ten minutes came a shock against the stern or side of the ship, which one would think should dash the planks in pieces."

While the memories of the storm were burned into Wesley's mind for the remainder of his life, it was what he saw in that group of Moravian Christians that changed him forever.

Wesley—who was himself afraid to die that day—later wrote of bloodcurdling screams and cries from the English passengers, but also of the continued singing of hymns by the German Christians, who, he recognized, had remained amazingly calm and at peace during the ordeal.

Later, after the storm had died down and everyone

aboard the *Simmonds* was safe, John Wesley asked one of the Moravians how they felt during the storm:

"Were you not afraid?"

"I thank God, no," came the answer.

"But were not your women and children afraid?" Wesley pressed.

"No," he replied, "our women and children are not afraid to die."

Later, Wesley made this incredible entry into his journal: "This was the most glorious day which I have hitherto seen."

In the midst of what was certainly a life-threatening crisis, John Wesley had witnessed the power of an unshakable faith in Jesus Christ, and it had a profound effect on him. From that time forward, he prayed regularly and asked God to grant him the kind of faith that would give him absolute confidence in God when he went through his own life storms.

God took John Wesley through a terrifying, life-threatening experience, and He did it for a reason: the perfecting of this great preacher's faith.

And He will allow us to go through life-shaking, sometimes life-*threatening*, storms in order to do the same thing for us.

God doesn't do this to bring about within us sinless perfection—none of us will achieve that this side of glory—but to cause us to grow and mature in our faith in Jesus Christ, to make us more like Him every day.

The apostle Peter, who went through two literal storms with his Lord as well as many other life storms as the founder of the church in Rome, spoke with great authority about the importance of our life storms when he wrote: "In this you greatly rejoice, though now for a little while you may have had to suffer grief in all kinds of trials. These have come so that your faith—of greater worth than gold, which perishes even though refined by fire—may be proved genuine and may result in praise, glory and honor when Jesus Christ is revealed" (1 Peter 1:6–7, NIV). George MacDonald, the Victorian novelist, poet, and fantasy writer, once wrote, "How often we look upon God as our last and feeblest resource! We go to Him because we have nowhere else to go. And then we learn that the storms of life have driven us, not upon the rocks, but into the desired haven."

The "desired haven" of which MacDonald wrote is Jesus Himself. When we endure life storms, we learn to rest and trust in the only One worthy of that kind of trust. Life storms. God uses them to move us and guide us to where He wants us. To shape us, change us, and make us more like Him. To draw us closer to Him. When we come to a place where we can praise Him and thank Him while in the very midst of a life storm, it will be time for God to move.

Time for a miracle!

"WHOM ARE YOU TALKING TO?"

On that awful, wonderful morning of waiting, worrying, and aloneness, I had nowhere to turn, no one to talk to but God Himself. With tears in my eyes and terrible fear in my heart, I prayed, "Lord, I feel so alone! No one is here; no one cares. There is no one here just to keep me company and talk while I wait!"

Then the Lord spoke to my heart so clearly and He said, "If you are so all alone, whom are you talking to?"

At that moment, I was face to face with the God who identified Himself in the last verse of the great prophecy of Ezekiel as "*Jehovah Shammah*," the name of the city, which translates to "the Lord is there" (Ezekiel 48:35). He is the God who is there.

While I sat in that waiting room, my heart was wracked with pain, fear, and worry. But in the midst of all that, I was comforted with the assurance that God was there for me, that He had a plan to do great things in Debbie's and my hearts through this terrible storm.

After what would be twelve hours of surgery that day, Debbie faced a long, difficult period of recovery —as well as several additional surgeries, some of them very difficult to endure. But through all of that, our God has been with us every step of the way, strengthening and perfecting our faith and helping us to rely on the incontrovertible fact that He alone is more than sufficient to meet all of our needs.

The twelve disciples of Christ indeed needed their faith in Jesus strengthened and perfected. He took them through a pair of fearsome storms to accomplish just that. They were about to see for themselves that no matter how severe the storm they faced, no matter how "alone" they felt, He would always be there for them.

That's a lesson Debbie and I have learned in a very real and very personal way. And that, maybe, should be "reason" enough for us: When the darkness falls and the storm rages, God stretches out His hand to draw us closer to Him.

CONSIDER THIS

Look back on a particularly hard time in your life. Is there any way you can honestly say you're grateful for those trials? Why or why not?

DIGGING DEEPER

Make a study of actual conversational exchanges between Jesus and the disciples. Note how He answers their questions. From this, imagine how He might answer questions you have.

CHAPTER FOUR

Mayday!

*Joy is not the absence of pain
but the presence of God.*

■ MOTHER TERESA

ON MARCH 1, 1939, THE United States military com-
missioned the U.S.S. *Squalus,* a then state-of-the-art attack
submarine. The Sargo-class sub, measuring 310 feet in
length, was a terror. It was to be a critical weapon in the
United States Navy's arsenal.

By late spring of that year, the *Squalus* had made
eighteen test dives, and all of them had gone smoothly
and successfully. But on its nineteenth test run, this one
thirteen miles southeast of the Piscataqua River, off the
coast of New Hampshire, disaster struck.

During the early morning hours of May 23, 1939, the
Squalus sank. A ventilation valve on the boat was opened
—due to either a mechanical or human error—allowing
water to rush into the submarine's rear compartments as
she descended. The *Squalus*'s entire back portion flooded,

almost instantly killing all twenty-six men in the ship's rear compartments. The rest of the crew—thirty-three men in all—were trapped in what they believed would become a steel coffin 243 feet below the surface.

The surviving crew released a messenger buoy and smoke bombs, hoping that someone would see them and send help. Nearly five hours later, the *Sculpin, Squalus's* sister ship, arrived, followed by rescue ships.

To conserve oxygen, the crew rested and waited. But their situation took another downward turn when seawater mixed with battery acid in the forward battery compartment, and chlorine gas began filling the compartment. The crew was able to protect themselves from the deadly gas by sealing off the battery compartment.

Now all they could do was wait . . . wait for their deaths . . . or for a miracle.

The remaining *Squalus* crew were wet, cold, and running out of oxygen. And they were well aware that no one had ever been successfully rescued from a sunken submarine.

The day after the *Squalus* sank, the submarine rescue vessel U.S.S. *Falcon* moored over the sunken ship. The rescue operation was led by Commander Charles "Swede" Momsen, who after the deaths of several of his friends in the sinking of a submarine in 1925 had designed the McCann rescue chamber, a large bell-shaped device which he hoped would be effective in the rescue mission.

The rescue crew knew they were entering uncharted territory. They knew that history contained no accounts of a successful rescue mission for a sunken submarine and that their mission might turn out to be another failed attempt. But still, they pressed forward, following Commander Momsen's orders to the letter.

A diver secured a cable near one of the *Squalus*'s escape hatches so that the diving bell could be guided to the submarine and back to the rescue ship. After four trips, the rescue team had completed its mission: All the survivors of the submarine accident had been miraculously rescued.

To this day, this mission is seen as the greatest submarine rescue in history.

Think about the men on the *Squalus*. Though a spectacular effort was being made to rescue them, they had to know that their chances still were not good. Though at some point they became aware that a rescue mission was underway, they also knew that nothing like this had been accomplished before.

I can't help but think that the disciples felt exactly as the men on the sunken *Squalus* felt. Out in the middle of the Sea of Galilee, with wind and waves pounding at them, they eventually lost their bearings and didn't know where they were going. They knew they were at the mercy of the elements. They must have wondered if that night was the night they would die.

THAT SINKING FEELING

Even in the best of conditions, even with a decent tailwind, rowing a boat across a miles-wide sea is hard, hard work. But what had been hard work that night became a frantic attempt on the disciples' part just to keep their boat on course. From everything we read in this story, it was a fruitless attempt.

The winds blowing over the sea were just too strong, and their boat had been blown back and forth, then off course. And, as if the wind and waves weren't fierce enough adversaries as these disciples "strained against the oars," three additional enemies arrived in turn: fatigue, fear, and discouragement.

Remember, the disciples had been up all day with Jesus, dealing with the needs and noise of thousands. Mark tells us that, originally, the time in the desolate place was supposed to be time away, away from the crowds. But the crowds found them, so they must have been weary even before they embarked on their journey across the sea. Likely they took turns at the oars. But as the wind kicked up and the waves began pounding the sides of the boat, what had been hard work became sheer torture. It wasn't long before they became so fatigued that they could barely make the effort to row.

Soon, fatigue turned to exhaustion, and exhaustion gave way to fear. The disciples, sapped of all physical strength, were now gripped with fear. They understood their situation. They were lost at sea, a storm was pounding at them, and they barely had the strength to grip the oars, let alone fight the wind and waves.

Finally, these exhausted, terrified disciples gave in to discouragement. They were discouraged because they were lost, discouraged because they couldn't row their boat, discouraged because Jesus wasn't there for them —at least not that they could see. Then the discouragement became a sort of resignation, an attitude that it was obviously their lot to die at sea that night and there was nothing they could do to change that fact.

Nearly all of us have had that "sinking" feeling at some point in our lives. That feeling of fatigue, fear, and discouragement that comes from knowing we are in a life storm and there is nothing we can do to change our situation. That feeling of dread, of wondering what is going to happen to us next. Or worse, just knowing that nothing good can come of our situation.

If you've ever been in a place in your life where you've lost a job, when your relationships are suffering, maybe even when you've feared for your life, you know the feeling. You expend enormous amounts of energy trying to save yourself, but it seems that nothing you do can help your situation.

You wonder if Jesus can see you, if He can do anything to calm the raging storms, both inside you and outside you.

THE GOD WHO SEES

On a hill overlooking the sea, Jesus was alone with the Father. As they had done for all of eternity past, they communed at a level far beyond human understanding. Jesus talked to His Father about how His mission to earth was progressing, about the miracles and teaching that had been a part of His day.

They talked about the people Jesus had touched and taught that day, and they talked about the disciples. In our limited human understanding, we might think that Jesus was praying for the disciples' safe arrival on the other side of the sea. But I believe He was praying for something else, something of far more importance in the eternal picture than a safe boat ride for the disciples. I believe Jesus was talking to the Father about this unique opportunity to teach the disciples something about who He really was.

Meanwhile, at that very moment, those same men, His followers and His friends, were in deep, deep trouble, in the middle of the lake, fighting a howling windstorm. They must have felt abandoned; they must have wondered what the Teacher was doing sending them out to sea at night. *He knew the treachery of the water. Why would He do such a thing? Why isn't He here with us?*

Then, miraculously, He saw them. In the middle of the night, with a storm blowing in over the sea, and from a fair distance from the mountain, He saw them, in trouble and straining at the oars.

But He also saw beyond the physical event. He knew what they were thinking, He knew the fear raging in their hearts. He knew they were wondering where He was and if He knew or cared what they were going through. He knew they were wondering if He was going to do anything about their desperate situation.

Not one small detail about the disciples' predicament had escaped Jesus' notice.

It's the same for us in our life storms. When we belong to Jesus, we are objects of His affection and compassion. We always have His attention, but even more so when we are being battered and beaten by a life storm.

Jesus sees what the man who has lost a job is going through. He sees what the family who is broke and facing the loss of their home is enduring. He sees what the cancer patient who faces surgery, chemotherapy, and a long and uncertain recovery faces. He sees what the parents whose child is rebelling and making their lives miserable have to withstand.

In the midst of all our sorrow, our fear, and our pain, Jesus sees us, and He not only cares, He is at the right hand of the Father interceding through it all. He not only cares, but He is working through these situations so that they bring us closer to Him and make us more like Him.

In the 139th Psalm, King David poses this rhetorical question: "Where can I go from your Spirit? Where can I flee from your presence?" David concludes that there is nowhere we can go where God can't see us, nowhere we can hide to get out of His presence. If we go to heaven He is there. If we try to hide in the darkness, He can see through it as if it were broad daylight.

A lot of people read into this passage a rather ominous message—that we'd better behave ourselves because God is always watching. Yes, the Lord knows all our thoughts and actions, both righteous and sinful. But this psalm is also a source of great comfort, for it assures us that no matter how dark the night, no matter how violent the storm, Jesus sees you as though it were a clear, sunny day.

But the story of this miracle scene also teaches us another wonderful truth about our Savior: Not only does He see us struggling and straining just to survive our life storms, but He also comes to us. He comes to us to bring rescue and comfort and to calm our fearful hearts.

A GHOST—OR GOD?

In the midst of their exhaustion, fear, and discouragement, the disciples see it. Approaching them through the wind-driven waves is a man-shaped figure. But something isn't right. It looks like a man all right, but there is no boat. As the figure draws closer, they see it but almost can't believe it.

He—or should we say "it"—is *walking on the water!*

But how could it be? Men don't just walk on the water, not even on calm water. The figure approaching them couldn't be a man!

The disciples couldn't take their eyes off the figure. Each and every one of these twelve men was frozen in terror at what they thought they were seeing. They couldn't move, couldn't speak. Finally one of them summoned the strength to say what the others were thinking.

"It's a ghost!"

Each of the men knew the tales that had become so much a part of the Jewish world. An old Jewish proverb warned that seeing a phantom at night was a prelude to disaster. They'd heard about what happened to sailors who had seen ghosts and phantoms on the water. They had heard that when a sailor saw something like that, it meant certain disaster. The disciples had all feared they were going to die at sea that night. But now they saw with their own eyes this harbinger of death.

With their hearts pounding, with certain death facing each one of them, the disciples did what they could to prepare themselves for what was coming. Then, through the noise of the wind and pounding water, they heard a voice calling out to them.

They knew that voice. They'd heard it deliver powerful sermons, heard it teach mightily, heard it order demons out of suffering people, heard it calm a storm with just three words.

It was the Master! Jesus knew what the disciples were going through. He knew they were filled with dread and fear over what was going on around them. He knew it was time for a miracle. Again, Jesus would perform a miracle using only words.

"Take courage," He called out. "It is I. Don't be afraid" (Mark 6:50, NIV).

Jesus came to these disciples in the darkest part of the night, in the deepest part of the sea. What was a hindrance for them was but a highway for Him. This shows us that nothing that hampers us hampers Him.

Mark makes a curious statement about this scene in Mark 6:48. He says that Jesus intended to pass them by. But what does that mean? Why would Jesus have gone out there just to pass them by?

In the Old Testament there are several references to God "passing by." In Exodus 33:19, 22 and in Exodus 34:6 God tells Moses, who asked to see God's glory, that He would cause His glory to pass by.

In 1 Kings 19:11 we read how Elijah stood at the mouth of a cave on Mount Horeb when the "Lord was passing by."

And in Job 9:8, 11, we read: "Who alone stretches out the heavens, and tramples down the waves of the sea . . . Were He to pass by me, I would not see Him; Were He to move past me, I would not perceive Him."

These Old Testament passages show us how God caused His glory to "pass by" those who were close to

Him. And Jesus is doing that very thing here. God in the flesh caused His glory to pass by these disciples so that they would see Him for who He truly was.

In but a moment, the storms of exhaustion, fear, and discouragement that had gripped these men's hearts disappeared into the wind. Their minds turned from their fear to a moment only days before when Jesus had rescued them from death.

The storm around the disciples raged on. The heavy wind and crashing waves continued pounding at the boat. But the storm within each of them ended instantly, leaving a calm and a peace like none the disciples had, just moments before, ever thought they would feel again. They had seen their Lord and heard His voice. Nothing could harm them now.

I can't help but think that the disciples did some celebrating at that moment. With the wind and waves still pounding at them, with their boat rocking so violently that water began spilling over the side, they shouted out with relief and joy, knowing they were going to be rescued.

Had it been up to the disciples, they would have missed their Savior that night, leaving themselves as lost and as doomed as they believed they were before He arrived on the scene. But Jesus went yet another step in calming his friends' hearts and nerves. In one gentle moment, He called out to them, "It is I; do not be afraid."

And in those times when our life storms become too heavy for us to bear, when we know that without a miracle we are sunk, He does the very same thing for us.

In the very midst of our heaviest life storms, in the midst of the deepest, darkest part of whatever we are going through, Jesus sees us, then approaches, walking on top of the very thing that pounds against us and has us paralyzed with fear. As He approaches, we often see Him through the lens of our storms, and we cry out in fear.

Sometimes when we are in the midst of a violent life storm, it's not easy to see Jesus. But, as the disciples learned, we can know that He is there for us, even in the worst of storms. But more than that, when we are so wrapped up in our fatigue, fear, even panic that we can't even see Him, He calls out to us.

It is I; do not be afraid!

When the disciples heard that familiar voice, they knew in their hearts that everything was going to be all right. They were going to live through that terrible night.

But for one of them, that wasn't enough. He wanted more.

KEEP WALKING!

The disciples had seen Jesus and heard His wonderful voice, and all inside them was calm. Calm despite the cold wind cutting through them and pushing their boat out of control. Calm despite the waves breaking against the side of the boat. Calm despite the fact that the storm that only moments before had them frightened and discouraged to the point of giving up continued raging on around them.

Before, when these terrified disciples called out to Jesus to save them from a storm, He simply spoke to the wind and water, and all was calm.

Not this time, though. Jesus was going to take the disciples another step in their faith. This time, His objective was to calm the storm inside these men while allowing the storm around them to continue raging on.

But why? Why not just calm the storm and be done with it? Why not just speak to the wind and water and make things quiet, then finish the night's journey?

Why? Because Jesus wasn't finished with this storm.

For Peter, just as for the others in the boat, hearing Jesus call out to him "It is I; do not be afraid" calmed his fears and put him at peace. But those words also inspired him. He wanted more than anything to step out of the boat, to experience a miracle all his own, a miracle that none of the other disciples dared ask for.

"Lord, if it is You, command me to come to You on the water," Peter called out.

At that moment, the other disciples must have thought Peter was some kind of lunatic. He'd always seemed a little "on the edge," but was he really asking what they thought he was asking? Did he *really* think it was possible for him to walk on the water?

That's exactly what he thought!

"Come!" Jesus called back, extending His hand to the disciple.

I have often wondered why Peter wanted to walk on the water, why he had the courage to ask Jesus to invite him. Was he showing off? Was he trying to impress the rest of the disciples—and Jesus Himself—with his faith? No, I believe Peter—that impetuous, passionate, easily excitable fisherman-turned-disciple—felt his spirits rise within him when he realized Jesus had arrived just in time to save him and his friends. At that moment, he felt within himself a passionate and un-quenchable desire to be where his Lord was.

At that moment, Peter was the only one of the twelve who had the kind of faith it took to actually suggest that he walk on the water.

So he made this one unthinkable request. *Just tell me it's You, and I'll come!*

By now, we all know what happened to Peter that night. With his heart pounding with excitement over what Jesus had called him to do, he stepped over the side of the boat and *onto* the water. With eleven men still in the boat, their eyes wide with wonder at what they were seeing, Peter began *walking on the water* toward his Lord.

But Peter, like a toddler taking his first few steps then losing his focus and falling down, took his eyes off Jesus. He looked away from his Lord and began focus-ing on the storm. When he saw the wind and waves, the excitement over what Jesus had called him to do was replaced with terror.

One moment, Peter was joyfully walking on water; the next, he was sinking into the sea like a stone and crying out for Jesus to save him.

Most of us love Peter's willingness to step out and his simple faith in approaching his Lord. But most of us can also identify with the fear that overtook Peter when he took his eyes off Jesus and began focusing on what was going on around him.

Most of us have been there. We have prayed about that new ministry, about that exciting business venture, about that relationship that seems so right—genuinely wanting to know God's will in the situation.

"Just tell me this is of You, and I'll step out," we earnestly pray.

Then we receive the green light, and we know in our hearts that God wants us to "step out of the boat," and move forward.

Then come the inevitable life storms, those bumps we are sure to encounter any time we attempt great things for God. Soon we are fearful, fatigued, discouraged, and feeling as if we are going to sink and drown if Jesus doesn't reach down and save us.

But if we want Jesus to do a miracle in our situations, we need to look beyond the storms and continue trusting. When Jesus tells us to step out of the boat and walk, we need to obey. And we need to do that, focusing not on our past failures or our present storms, but on Him. And when the wind begins to push us around and the waves begin lapping at our feet, we need to do one thing: keep walking!

Jesus performed a series of miracles for the disciples that night, all of which showed the disciples and us some things we need to know about Him when we are in the midst of a life storm and needing a miracle:

*On a clear day, when everything is calm and you can see
Me clearly, you can trust Me.*

*On a stormy day, when you can't see past the wind,
waves, and rain and see Me, you can trust Me.*

*And on a stormy day, when you choose to step out in faith
expecting a miracle—despite what you see going on
around you—you can most certainly trust Me.*

CONSIDER THIS

Whether you are in the midst of a storm or your life
is relatively calm right now, you need to keep your eyes
on Jesus. But what does that actually mean in terms of
day-to-day living, choices, thoughts, and actions? What
would your life look like if you kept your eyes on Jesus
at all times?

DIGGING DEEPER

Do a study of events in Scripture that happen
specifically so God's power may be displayed.

CHAPTER FIVE

OPENING BLIND EYES

I should not be a Christian but for the miracles.

■ AUGUSTINE OF HIPPO

AS A CHILD, DID you ever play the party game called "Blind Man's Bluff?"

There are several variations of Blind Man's Bluff. In one variation, a player—the one who is "It"—is blindfolded, placed in the middle of a circle of players, and spun around five times while the other players scatter and find places to hide in the yard where they play. When the player who is "It" finishes the fifth spin, the other players must freeze in place. "It" then calls out "Blind Man's . . ." and the other players answer by yelling ". . . Bluff," trying to hide their location and identity by disguising their voices.

The object of the game is for the player who is "It" to use the senses of hearing and touch to track down and identify his or her friends while in complete physical darkness. It isn't as easy as it may sound!

The apostle John records in his gospel the story of a man who was in that kind of darkness, who had to rely on senses other than sight in order to function in the world around him. For this man, however, this wasn't a mere child's game. It had been his entire real life. And it was a life changed through an encounter with a miracle worker by the name of Jesus Christ.

THE LIGHT AT THE FEAST

Jesus was in Jerusalem—the scene of the meeting with the blind man—during a celebration known as the Feast of Tabernacles. It was the final feast of the year and a time when the Jews commemorated God's provision for their ancestors during their forty-year sojourn in the wilderness during the time of the Exodus.

At the end of the first day of this festival, several golden lamps were placed near the temple and lit, creating a warm glow around the temple. With the Light from these lamps flickering in His face, Jesus turned to some Jewish religious authorities and made what was to them a very provocative statement: "I am the Light of the world; he who follows Me will not walk in the darkness, but will have the Light of life" (John 8:12).

This was the first of many assertions by Jesus that had the Pharisees looking for a reason to kill Him. They had already tried to bait Him into saying something for which they could arrest Him. They had just brought before Him an adulterous woman—a woman caught in the very act—and asked Him whether they should follow Jewish law to the letter and stone her to death. Jesus not only showed this sinful woman mercy and sent her away forgiven and cleansed; He reminded the Pharisees that they—as pious and religious as they thought themselves to be—were still sinful human beings.

Of course, the Pharisees were none too pleased to hear this. They responded by throwing accusations and leading questions at Jesus, hoping to trip Him up.

But Jesus didn't back down. In the face of all the questioning and testing and accusations, He held firm in speaking the truth of who He was. Finally, Jesus got down to the ultimate truth of who He was: "I tell you the truth, . . . before Abraham was born, I am!" (John 8:58 NIV).

The Pharisees had heard enough. In their minds, this man was a blasphemer and deserved to die on the spot. So they picked up stones to throw at Him.

When the time was right, the Jewish religious leaders would get their shot at Jesus, but not today. It wasn't the time His Father had appointed for Him to suffer and die. Jesus hid from the Pharisees and left the temple.

Now, with Jesus' proclamation that He was the light of the world still fresh in the minds of the disciples and other witnesses, Jesus went from telling who He was to *showing* them.

IMAGINE SUCH A LIFE . . .

As Jesus left the temple, He fixed His gaze on one man. Many people were coming and going that day, all of them with their own needs and their own life struggles. But the man who caught Jesus' eye at that one moment was one with a need different from any other. The man was totally blind.

He had been born blind and had spent every day since then living in complete physical darkness. He lived in a time and a place when the world had little use for a blind man, so he could do nothing more than sit in the streets of Jerusalem and beg. Some gave to him, but most ignored him and went their way.

This is the only place in Scripture where we read of a man who had been blind his whole life. The term in the Greek is *ekgennesis*, which means "out of the genesis—or beginning—of life." He had never seen a sunrise or sunset. Words such as *bright, shiny, blue*, or *green* meant nothing to him. He had never seen the streets of Jerusalem, busy with people coming and going. He had never seen another human being. He had never even seen his own mother's face.

The man lived in a world most of us can't begin to understand. Even if you or I were to suddenly lose our sight, we would have a point of reference for what the word *sight* meant. We would at least have some memory of seeing. The man was not only sightless; he didn't even know what sight was. He not only lived in darkness; he didn't even know what the word *light* meant.

Having lived his entire life without sight, this man had learned to get around and function well enough

in the world around him that he was able to beg
enough to keep him alive. To him, this was what "normal" life was like. He knew of no other way.

But into this man's world of darkness walked
Jesus, who saw his condition and felt compassion for
him. Compassion because he had lived his whole life
in total darkness. Compassion because he lacked one
of the basic necessities of life. Compassion because he
probably didn't even know of his own need.

Jesus had a plan that day, a plan to do the miraculous for this man. He also had a lesson for the disciples and others who were about to witness this miracle.

WHOSE FAULT?

When the disciples first saw the blind man, they
asked a very interesting but very misguided question
about this man's physical blindness: "Rabbi, who
sinned, this man or his parents, that he would be born
blind?" (John 9:2).

The premise of the question wasn't *whether* someone had done wrong and caused the man's blindness
but *whose* sin had caused it. The disciples' question
reflected the age-old debate and teaching among the
religious leaders in Jewish circles about evil and suffering.

The religious authorities at the time of Christ's
earthly ministry held different theories as to why
people suffered, why some were born with physical
problems, and why people became sick or crippled.
One of those theories was based on the story of the
birth of Jacob and Esau, the twin sons of Isaac and

Rebekah, as recorded in the book of Genesis. Esau was born first, but Jacob came right behind, holding on to his brother's heel at the moment he entered the world (see Genesis 25:25–26).

The assumption on the part of some rabbis was that Jacob and Esau had been battling one another while still in the womb, that Jacob was actually trying to kill Esau as the two were born. This led them to believe that an unborn child could commit "prenatal" sin.

With the disciples awaiting an answer, Jesus moved the discussion to a different plane. He didn't talk to them about whose sin caused the man's blindness or even what sin had to do with it. He didn't talk to them about the part the "original sin"—Adam and Eve's rebellion in the Garden of Eden—played in human suffering. Jesus knew better than any of the disciples that sin was the sole reason humans had to suffer and die. He knew that without that act of rebellion committed many millennia before, there would be no sickness, no blindness, no lameness, and no death.

But Jesus also knew that God had placed this man who had been in darkness since birth so He could demonstrate to the disciples and to others who He was and what He could do.

Jesus didn't scold the disciples for their lack of understanding. Rather, He simply corrected their thinking and prepared them to understand the meaning for what was about to happen: "It was neither that this man sinned, nor his parents; but it was so that the works of God might be displayed in him" (John 9:3).

From the very start of this miracle scene, Jesus was teaching. His lesson for the disciples—and for us today—was this: Sometimes human suffering isn't as much a result of our own sin as it is an opportunity for God to be glorified for the world to see.

WHY, LORD?

I believe we have all struggled with the question of why we suffer and go through storms and trials in our lives. Just as the disciples looked at this blind man and wondered what caused his sightlessness, we look at our own situation, our own storms and trials, and wonder "*Why?*"

Why have I lost my job and my ability to provide for my family?

Why is my marriage falling apart, and it seems there is nothing I can do about it?

Why has my child rebelled and brought my family and me so much anguish?

Why must I suffer through this terrible illness?

Why me?

It is human nature when we are going through some hurt or tragedy to want God to give us a full and detailed explanation of why it's happening to us. We wonder if it's something we've done or haven't done that has brought this trial on us. So we look toward heaven and ask "Why?" then wait—most of the time not too patiently—for an answer we are sure will come.

Sometimes God answers those questions quickly

and specifically. Sometimes He lets us know it's a matter of His teaching us some life lesson we needed to learn. Sometimes it's a matter of God allowing a trial or tragedy to come our way to smooth away our rough edges, much the same way a potter uses the implements of his trade to smooth away the flaws in a piece of artwork. And sometimes it's a matter of God bringing tough times to correct us or to create within us what the psalmist called a "clean heart" (Psalm 51:10).

At times, God answers these questions. But sometimes, instead of an answer, our questions concerning our suffering are met with silence.

But why? In the midst of the darkness of our personal struggles, why does our heavenly Father remain silent when we ask Him the reason for our suffering?

I believe it may be because often we ask the wrong questions.

I wonder how much difference it would make in the inner lives of those who are going through life crises if they would ask not "Why?" but "What?"

"*What* great things can God do through my own situation?"

"*What* can God teach me through this suffering and turmoil?"

"*What* kind of *miracle* will God perform through all of this?"

The apostle Paul made this very point when he wrote, "And we *know* that God *causes* all things to work together for good to those who love God, to those who are called according to His purpose" (Romans 8:28, italics added).

A lot of believers have taken this verse to mean that everything will work out, that God will somehow take our trials, storms, and tests and miraculously turn them around and relieve us of our suffering. But that's not what Paul was saying. Instead, he was saying that even if we have to continue in our suffering, He can do great things in the very midst of it.

That's a bold, confident statement on the part of the apostle. It assures us we can know that no matter what kind of pain we face, God will do something good —not necessarily about it, but through it.

When in the midst of our pain we cry out to God, He doesn't always come with an instant explanation. Sometimes He doesn't come with an explanation at all. But when we put our faith in Him, He comes right into tragedy and our hurt and uses it as an opportunity to bring us out of our darkness and further into His light.

THE TRUTH ABOUT BLINDNESS

Jesus' encounter with this blind man was not only a moment for Him to express His identity as the Son of God and the power that identity holds. It was also a chance for Him to teach us a vitally important spiritual truth: We are all "blind from birth."

In one very real way, each human being is just like this man who had been born blind. From the moment we are born, we all walk in spiritual darkness. None of us had to "learn" to be sinners. Why? Because regardless of who we are or where we live we all are born with the sin nature.

We're also like the man born blind in that we

don't even realize we are living in darkness. Just as physical darkness was all this man had ever known, spiritual darkness was all we knew before we came to Christ.

That brings us to the most important truth behind what Jesus was about to do for this man born blind, and it's this: He not only is aware of our darkness, but He also longs to walk into the darkness each of us lives in and bring light. Only through the miraculous touch of the Savior are our eyes opened so we can see our need for Him and then respond to His offer to bring us into the light.

This is exactly the opposite of what our world teaches today. The New Age Movement teaches that man himself is light, while other religions—even some based (however loosely) on the Christian faith—believe that man, while he is born in darkness, is ever changing and improving and moving toward some kind of spiritual light. Still other belief systems state that we all have an "inner light" and all we need is something to bring it out.

But in this miracle scene, Jesus demonstrated a truth about His relationship to humanity, one contrary to what many of the world's belief systems teach: We are born in spiritual darkness, and unless He comes in and sheds His light on us, we continue to walk in that darkness for our whole lives.

Now, with this blind man before Him, Jesus was going to demonstrate that spiritual truth through a physical healing.

A MUDDY MIRACLE

When Jesus saw the blind man near the temple, He knew of this poor soul's need. The Bible doesn't tell us whether the man said anything to Jesus, just that he had a need and that, in the midst of that need, Jesus reached out to him and gave.

With the blind man sitting before Him and the disciples and others looking on, Jesus did something very curious, something completely unlike anything He had done for anyone else. He spat on the ground and made mud of the spit and dirt. Then He took the mud and smeared it on the blind man's eyes.

The disciples had never seen Him do anything quite like that. Sure, they'd seen Him do amazing miracles. They'd seen Him turn water to wine, feed thousands with five small loaves of bread and a couple of puny fish, and calm storms with just His words. They'd seen Him walk on water and heal sick and crippled people.

But they'd never seen Him do anything like this.

Those who witnessed this scene must have wondered what Jesus was thinking. Here was this poor blind man who could do nothing more to get by in life than beg for handouts, and all Jesus did for him was muddy up his face.

I've often wondered myself why Jesus chose to perform this miracle. Why not just touch the man and pronounce him healed? Why not just make him a seeing man with just a word?

Over the centuries, there have been countless explanations and theories as to why Jesus made this bit of mud with His spit then put it on the blind man's eyes. Some have said He did it because human saliva was believed to have some kind of curative power. Others have held that Jesus needed time to heal this man's eyes. (Of course, that would have been the one and only time recorded in the Gospels where Jesus "needed" time to perform a miracle!) Still others have held that perhaps the man wasn't totally blind and Jesus wanted to make him so before healing him. Still others see the clay as a metaphor for our humanity.

Personally, I have no idea why Jesus chose to begin this miracle the way He did. What I do know is that Jesus met this man where he was living—in a world of total and complete darkness—and reached out His hand and performed the one miracle this man needed.

I have concluded that Jesus' making the mud out of some dust and His spit, then putting it on this man's face, aren't the important part of this story, that they probably don't hold any real meaning for us today. The important part of the story—the one part each of us who needs or will need a miracle in the future needs to see—was what happened after Jesus put the mud on the blind man's eyes.

OBEDIENCE: OUR PART IN GOD'S MIRACLES

After smearing this man's until-now useless eyes with mud, Jesus told him to go and wash his face in the pool of Siloam (John 9:7).

Now, the blind man had a decision to make.

When Jesus told the man to go to the pool of

Siloam and wash his eyes, he could have refused. He could have simply told Him, "No, I won't do it!" In a way, that might have been understandable. After all, this was a man who didn't know what sight was, and he didn't have full understanding of what Jesus wanted to do for him. Besides, what Jesus had done to him already must have struck him as really strange if not downright crazy.

Jesus sent the man to the pool of Siloam, which means "sent." This was water "sent" by God. John in his Gospel is constantly showing Jesus as the "sent" one. This very well may have something to do with why Jesus smeared mud in the blind man's eyes—so that the "sent" One could send this man to the waters sent from God for cleansing.

But would he go? Would he act in "blind" obedience?

He obeyed and did as Jesus had told him to do, and he did it not even knowing what sight was. This was for him a step of obedience that would bring the miracle to completion.

And it's a step each of us who needs Jesus to perform a miracle for us needs to take.

The blind man with the muddy face made his way to the pool, bent down with his face over the water, scooped the water onto his face, and washed away the mud. Then, the miracle was complete. He could see!

It's hard for those of us with sight to imagine the awe and wonder this man must have felt when he first saw.

He looked in front of him and saw for the first time his own hands, the same hands he had for so many years held out in hopes of receiving gifts from strangers. He looked down into the pool and saw the ripples and the sun splashing on the water. He looked up and saw blue sky and fluffy, white clouds. Then he looked around him and saw the people who before had been just voices speaking to one another and occasionally to him.

I can imagine the man just kneeling at the water's edge taking it all in with his newly functioning eyes, feeling a mixture of wonder and joy—and maybe a little fear—over the "new" world that had opened up before him.

Then, his heart jumped as he realized there was something—someONE—he had to see. He hurriedly got up from the pool and made his way back to where he had met the man who had done such a peculiar thing to him, but who also had given him a gift like none he had any way of imagining—at least until that day.

John records that the man went away from Jesus blind but came back to Him seeing (see John 9:7). We can only imagine the wonder he felt at seeing the One who did for him what no one else could, or what no one else had cared enough to do.

And all he had to do to receive this miracle was one small act of obedience.

There were some underlying messages behind what Jesus did for this man who had been blind from the day he was born. Just as this man's physical blindness represents spiritual darkness, so this washing of his eyes points toward spiritual cleansing, the kind of cleansing only He can do. Just as the blind man's obedience was an essential part of this miracle of Jesus, so is our obedience essential when we want Him to perform a miracle in our lives.

So many believers today are looking for miracles. Miracles at work, miracles in their families, miracles in their physical bodies, miracles in their personal lives. But while they are looking for miracles, they have left out of their own lives Jesus' one condition for the miracle He performed for this man: obedience.

Sadly, many professing Christians spend so much of their lives in disobedience that they become blind and desensitized when it comes to hearing God's Word and responding. They have done many of the things God has asked them to do, but they have neglected or refused to do others. Yes, they'll get to heaven someday. But only after missing out on many of God's blessings—many of His *miracles*—meant for them in this present life.

Dietrich Bonhoeffer, the World War II-era German theologian and pastor who was imprisoned by Adolf Hitler at the concentration camp at Flossenburg and then hanged by orders of Hitler himself, said this of obedience to Christ: "You can only know that you are believing because you are obeying and you can only know that you are obeying because you are believing."

Indeed, a bone-and-marrow kind of connection links obedience, faith, and miracles. Without obedience there is no life-changing faith, and without faith there are no miracles.

In short, if we want God to do miracles, we need to walk in obedience.

Have you been waiting for God to do a miracle in your life? Waiting for weeks, months, maybe years—and nothing seems to be happening?

Perhaps it's a matter of obedience.

Maybe God is asking you to give up some sinful habit. Maybe He's asking you to be reconciled to a family member or to a brother or sister in Christ. Maybe He's just asking you simply to step out in faith and share your faith with someone in your sphere of influence. And maybe, just maybe, He's asking you to move into a fuller and deeper relationship with Him by spending more of your valuable time in His presence through prayer, praise, and time in the Word.

Whatever God is calling you to do, if you want Him to do a miracle in your life, you need to do it.

When Jesus told the blind man to go and wash, he went and washed, and because of this act of obedience, he was blessed and healed in a way far beyond anything he dared dream of or expect. Jesus demonstrated His power to bring man out of the midnight of darkness and into His light.

The same can be true for us today, if we only respond to Jesus in obedience.

When we first come to Christ in obedience, we're much like that blind man who had never enjoyed the sense of sight. Before Jesus, we had no idea what real light was. But when He brings us from our personal darkness and into His light, it's a completely new experience for us, so new and so wonderful that we can't find words to describe it.

I've had the chance to minister to and meet with many people who have come from darkness many of us can't begin to understand, people who had spent every day of their lives engaged in every kind of sin and rebellion imaginable. They go through life in utter and complete darkness. But then, for the first time in their lives, their spiritual eyes are opened. They see Jesus.

It's hard for me to put into words the joy I felt when I saw the wonder and awe these people expressed once they obeyed and gave the whole of themselves to Christ. They had come to Jesus in simple obedience, without any preconceived notions about what He intended to do for them—outside of forgiving their sins and assuring them a place in heaven. But once they responded to Jesus in obedience, He miraculously filled them with a peace and a joy beyond anything they could have comprehended.

For them, just as for the blind man Jesus healed, it was a whole new world.

Sadly, many "veterans of the faith" have lost that peace and joy. They no longer walk consistently in the light of Jesus Christ. Their hearts feel dead, and their once-vibrant faith seems only a faint memory. Oftentimes, this is because they missed something somewhere along the way, maybe because they have failed to obey what may be a very simple command from their Lord. Because of that, they live their lives playing a spiritual version of "Blind Man's Bluff," unable to see or experience the blessings God has for them.

The good news is that Jesus knows our hearts and what we are going through. He desires more than anything to reopen our spiritual eyes and allow us once again to enjoy the light He came to bring us.

Our Lord wants to bless us and to do true miracles in our lives. But we've got to do our part in allowing Him to do those miracles. That's obedience. When we humbly obey our Lord and give Him everything we have and everything we are, He'll perform for us the greatest miracle of all.

We'll see Jesus!

CONSIDER THIS

Many people today suffer from spiritual "blindness." How can you use your "clay," your humanity, to help open their eyes?

DIGGING DEEPER

Do a study of the "I am" statements Jesus made, particularly in John. Then use them as part of your personal prayer time, praising Him with "You are . . ."

AFTER THE MIRACLE . . .

*Miracles are a retelling in small
letters of the very same story which is
written across the whole world in
letters too large for some of us to see.*

■ C. S. LEWIS

HOW DO WE KNOW when something's a miracle?

Today we throw around the term rather loosely. Everything from a come-from-behind victory for our favorite underdog team to a newborn baby to a maple leaf in autumn to finding our misplaced car keys seems to qualify.

But it hasn't always been that way. Perhaps in an effort to downplay "superstition," there have been times when the church minimized the role of miracles. Christians acknowledged that God was to some extent active in the church and in the world around us, but asserted that, for the most part, there were logical, rational explanations for the events that previous generations had seen as miraculous.

Certainly not every great occurrence is a miracle. Sometimes, God sends us out to do things for His kingdom, and it's because of our obedience and our doing the work He has put before us that great things happen. But I also know that there are times when it is only through a direct act of God—what I call a miracle— and not any kind of human effort or "coincidence" that good things happen.

Certainly, we all need to seek balance when it comes to deciding for ourselves what is and isn't a miracle. While we need to be careful not to label everything a "miracle," we also need to be careful not to miss the miraculous when it happens in front of us.

Which is exactly what happened to some people John tells us about.

MISSING THE MIRACULOUS?

After stopping and taking the time to heal the man who had spent his whole life in absolute darkness, Jesus went on His way. There was more teaching, more work, and more miracles for Him to perform.

But there were also things for the newly seeing man to see, say, and do. The man, who until that day hadn't even seen his own hands in front of his face, went back to his home and to his family, friends, and neighbors—the people who had known him all of his life.

That must have been quite a scene!

I can't help but think that the man beamed with excitement and wonder over the fact that he could see, that for the first time in his existence he actually experienced for himself the sense of sight. For the first time, he made his way through the city using his sight and not just his senses of hearing and touch and a walking stick. And for the first time, he actually *saw* the people he had known all his life.

At first, the people's reaction to finding out that this blind man could see was mixed. Some of them *knew* beyond a doubt that it was he and were astonished. But others weren't so sure. They believed it was possible they weren't even looking at the same man, just someone who looked a lot like him but who'd had his sight all along.

Of course, there were questions. Lots of questions.

"WHO DID THIS?"

Can you imagine what would happen today if a well-known blind person were to suddenly receive sight? I can imagine the media frenzy that would take place if, for example, pop singer Stevie Wonder were to announce that someone had miraculously given him the ability to see. Reporters from all over the world would look for chances to talk to the star and ask him what had happened, how it happened, and who did it.

Although it must have been on a smaller scale, that is what happened after Jesus gave the man born blind sight. John doesn't record everything the people at the scene asked the man, but I don't doubt that they had a wide variety of questions for him. I know that if I met a man who had been the object of such a miracle I'd want to know not only what happened, how it happened, and who caused it to happen, but what it was like to see for the first time in his life. Was he excited? Scared? What was he going to do next?

That's what happens when Jesus brings someone

out of darkness into the light—like when He transforms us into something we weren't before. People ask questions. They want to know what has happened to change us and who was responsible. They want details. They want to know our feelings and what we will do next, now that we've been changed by the love of Christ.

The man Jesus healed of his lifelong blindness saw many things that first day. In his heart and mind, he "saw" something we who have been transformed by Jesus Christ need to understand: With this new "seeing" comes responsibility, the responsibility of telling others who have questions what has happened to make us so "different" from what we were before.

John tells us that this man who had received from Jesus the gift of sight *repeatedly* told his neighbors that it was indeed he who had been blind and that now he could indeed see. I am sure this man didn't grow tired of telling them that they could believe their own eyes, that they were in fact looking at the same man they had seen begging earlier that very day.

Probably most of the people who had wondered if it was really he came away from their questioning satisfied that he really was the same man who, the very day before the miracle, had been a blind beggar. And when they were sure it was he, they started asking the next logical question people ask when someone who had been blind from birth suddenly gained sight: *How* did this happen?

The man could hardly keep quiet about what had happened and who had done it for him. He enthusiastically told them of the strange but wonderful events surrounding this miracle: "The man they call Jesus made some mud and put it on my eyes. He told me to go to Siloam and wash. So I went and washed, and then I could see" (John 9:11 NIV).

Then came the natural response to the man's explanation for what had happened. The people wanted to know where this Jesus was at that moment. They wanted to see Him for themselves, to meet Him and see what He could do for them. After all, if He was able to do this for a man who had been blind his whole life, there was no telling what other kinds of miracles He could perform on their behalf.

This account of a miracle of Jesus demonstrates something else we all need to remember: When meeting Jesus so profoundly changes us, it gets people's attention. They see the difference in our lives, in our attitudes, and in our hearts, and they want to know what caused it and, oftentimes, if what changed us can change them too.

When this man's neighbors realized what had happened, they wanted to know details. They wanted to know what happened, how it happened, and who did it—and they wanted to meet Jesus.

It would have seemed like an occasion for the blind man's family and neighbors—and religious leaders—to celebrate, but if they had any such inclination, the spoilers among them had other priorities. They missed the opportunity for celebration, as we so often do in the church.

From the first word of the Old Testament through

the last word of the New, the Word of God shows us that the kingdom of God is all about celebration. It's the kind of celebration that you might expect to break out when the blind man's friends and family realized that he could now see. And it's the kind of celebration the world around us needs to see.

A church in the Kings Cross section of Sydney, Australia—in the "red light" district—understands and practices this kind of celebration every week. Each and every Sunday morning, the congregation meets at 8:00 for a time of intensive prayer and praise. Then, with the Spirit of God moving within them, they head out into the streets to meet with people who need Jesus Christ—with prostitutes, with street people, with runaways, with those who wake up every morning disappointed and disillusioned with life.

These believers take anyone who is willing out for breakfast or for coffee, and they talk to them about Jesus. They wind up their morning with an 11:15 celebration service, oftentimes bringing with them the people they just took to breakfast. When one of those people makes a decision to follow Jesus Christ, this church breaks into a celebration like the one Jesus talked about in Luke 15:7: "I tell you . . . there will be more joy in heaven over one sinner who repents than over ninety-nine righteous persons who need no repentance."

That is a church that understands the blessings behind celebrating the kingdom of God. A church that understands that allowing others to see their joy in Christ helps them to see His kind of light. It's a church where miracles happen!

I believe that should be the look of all of God's churches. Too many church services are dry, boring, and unemotional. We've forgotten that Jesus has given us cause for celebration, forgotten that when we get together in His name we are to celebrate who He is and what He's done for us, forgotten to celebrate the miraculous.

Once we learn to focus on Jesus and to recognize a miracle on His part, then our lives will reflect an attitude of celebration much like the one about to break out at the miracle scene recorded in the ninth chapter of John.

MISSING THE POINT

When the man's friends got word of what had happened, they did something many would consider a mistake: They took him to the Pharisees.

If you know anything about Pharisees, you know that one sure way to kill a celebration over such an amazing event is to tell them about it. The Pharisees were a legalistic bunch, so focused on their rules, regulations, and religion that they had lost their ability to truly see God, to have any kind of personal relationship with Him, or to recognize a miracle when they saw it.

The Bible doesn't tell us specifically why the people took the formerly blind man to the Pharisees. Some have read into these people's actions that they wanted the Pharisees to know that Jesus had done this "work" on the Sabbath so that they could correct the situation—like they were "tattling" on Jesus. Or possibly, they were all caught up in the celebration of this miracle, and they wanted the only spiritual leaders they had ever known to explain to them what had happened and what it meant.

But the Pharisees, those wet blankets in religious garb, weren't as interested in what Jesus had done for this man as much as they were concerned about *when* He did it. If Jesus had healed this man on the Sabbath—and He clearly did—then He had broken one of their rules. Now, the Pharisees wanted answers.

The first thing the Pharisees asked the man was what had happened. As he had done when his friends and neighbors had asked the same question, he cheerfully told them about the man called Jesus, about the mud, about the washing, and about the new world opened up before him.

That is when this scene takes a somewhat humorous turn. John records how the Pharisees—despite the testimony of witnesses and despite what they saw before them—had a difficult time taking a position on what had happened. No, they didn't focus on the fact that this man who was blind could now see but on whether the work was done legally. Talk about totally missing the point! Some of them said that since Jesus healed this man on the Sabbath, then He broke their law and was therefore a sinner. But others in the group held that if He could do a miracle like giving a man blind from birth sight, then there was no way He could be a sinner.

Clearly this was a dilemma. There these Pharisees

were, with this common man in their presence and talking about the miracle work Jesus had done, and they couldn't agree on what they should think about what had happened. They needed to clear up the situation, and they needed to do it fast. So in order to reach some kind of agreement among themselves, they simply decided to refuse to accept the fact that the man had ever been blind in the first place.

Their reasoning bordered on the absurd. It was "circular reasoning" at its worst. These learned religious leaders held that if Jesus healed this man, then clearly He was a righteous man, but they also held that He couldn't have been a righteous man while breaking the Sabbath. Therefore, the man Jesus allegedly healed couldn't have been blind in the first place.

In short, the man who had spent his whole life begging near the temple because his lack of sight prevented him from finding meaningful work must have been faking his disability. Therefore, the "miracle" was really nothing more than a ruse on the part of Jesus.

It is amazing how far these "religious" men went to maintain their disbelief. They had already heard Jesus' teaching and heard accounts—if not witnessed personally—about some of His many miracles in the city. Yet to justify or affirm their own disbelief, they choose instead to believe the ridiculous. It is obvious that they did not care about the man born blind, and it is also obvious that they were going to reject Christ as Messiah even if it meant believing something so obviously untrue.

The tragedy of this scene is that while Jesus did a wonderful miracle almost right in front of the Pharisees' eyes, they could not recognize it because of their rules and laws, as well as their preconceived notions of what they believed about the coming Messiah. They had missed the miraculous—and they had missed the Messiah.

THE WET BLANKETS AMONG US

Some Christians today are very much like those Pharisees. They may not try to discount or disprove who Jesus is, but they always find something to complain about or ways to diminish or downplay something God is doing in the life of another believer or in the body of Christ.

Just as the witnesses taking the formerly blind man to the Pharisees killed that celebration, so does taking the testimony of a miracle or other move of God to people with these kinds of attitudes throw water on the fire the Lord has started. They are, in fact, people who will go out of their way to look for reasons not to believe in the miraculous.

Why do some of us do that, even as God does great things right out in the open for us to see?

Sometimes it's a matter of treating our "religion" the way the Pharisees did: as a list of rules and not a relationship with the living God. Others of us have been disappointed with fellow followers of Christ, and it has made us cynical. Some of us are secretly struggling with an unconfessed sin. Still others simply have never come to fully understand God's wonderful grace. We walk around with a cloud of sin and guilt over our heads, not realizing that God's grace means immediate cleansing and forgiveness when we come to Him in humble confession.

Do you want to see the miraculous in your own life? Then you may need to change your focus. Instead of focusing on religion and rules, focus on your personal relationship with God through Jesus Christ. Instead of focusing on your own sinful desires, focus on the life God has for you. And instead of focusing on your own shortcomings, focus on the God whose grace is more than enough to cover your every sin.

So often because we are focused on everything else, we miss the miraculous and what God is doing.

Hawa Ahmed was a Muslim student in North Africa.[1] One day she was reading a Christian tract in her dorm room and under conviction received Jesus Christ as her Lord and Savior. Her father was an Emir (Islamic ruler) so she expected her family to be upset, but she had no idea that her family would react the way they did. When she shared with them about her conversion and that she had changed her name to Faith, her father exploded with rage. Her father and brothers stripped her naked and tied her to a metal chair. They intended to electrocute her.

She asked if they would place her Bible in her lap which they did. Sitting there in that horrible situation she focused on God's word and felt a peace, as though someone was standing by her. Her father and brothers pushed the plug into the socket, but nothing happened. They tried it again. Then they tried it with a different cable. Finally in frustration they threw her naked out of the house and into the street.

Faith ran through the streets naked, humiliated, and in pain. She ran to the home of a friend who let her in, gave her some clothes, and provided her a place to stay. The next day Faith's friend asked some neighbors what they thought because they had seen Faith running naked through the streets. "What are you talking about?" they asked. "The girl had on a beautiful white dress. We asked ourselves why someone so beautifully clothed would be running through the streets."

God obviously had hidden her nakedness from their eyes. Faith is now serving with the ministry Every Home for Christ.

In those moments of fear and terror Faith focused on her relationship with God, and God met her needs. When you begin to focus on Christ, not on your circumstances or the situation around you, you will not only sense His presence but experience the deliverance that only He can bring. It might not be as dramatic as Faith's experience. It might not be some spectacular experience like the blind man receiving his sight. It might not be not be some dazzling deliverance like Daniel in the lion's den, but we are assured by God's word that in quietness and trust we will experience strength (Isaiah 30:15).

In May 2002, Leonardo Diaz, a Colombian hiker, decided to go mountain climbing with some friends. Their goal was to reach the summit of the Nevado del

Ruiz, a volcano in the Andes. [2]

On the second day of the climb, a major blizzard hit. Diaz lost sight of his friends, and became separated from them. After a period of time he began to run out of rations and started to suffer from the cold.

He remembered that he had a cell phone in his backpack but his pre-paid minutes had expired. With no way to find his friends, and no way to call for help, he realized he was not going to make it.

He lay in the frigid snow preparing to die when all of a sudden his cell phone rang. It was a telemarketer wanting to know if he was interested in purchasing more minutes! "We called him to remind him that he was out of minutes," said Maria del Pilar Bastos of Bell South.

Diaz knew that God had moved in a miraculous way. The Bell South operator could tell that he was beginning to suffer from hypothermia and kept him on the phone, got his location, and called for rescuers with the information. Seven hours later Diaz was found, and rescuers brought him to safety.

In the everyday things God moves in miraculous ways. You can't convince Leonardo Diaz that God does not use the usual in an unusual way to move in our lives. Sometimes we are simply too blind to see the hand of God, the deliverance of God, the ways of God. Sometimes we have to be desperate before we see the miraculous. But once our eyes are opened, we can see God moving everywhere.

"THIS MAN"

The Pharisees who questioned the man born blind went out of their way to miss the miraculous. They questioned him about what happened, then came to their own conclusion—as backward and upside-down in its thinking as it was—concerning what had happened that day.

But the Pharisees took their unbelief several more steps. After questioning the man, they went to his parents, who confirmed that he was their son, that he had been blind from birth, and that now he could see. But if they wanted to know anything more, the man's mother and father told the Pharisees, they'd have to ask him themselves.

That's exactly what they did.

The Pharisees summoned this formerly blind man a second time in their hope of trapping him and getting him to say something they could use to accuse Jesus. "Give glory to God," they told him, "we know that this man is a sinner" (John 9:24).

It's no accident that the Pharisees refused to call Jesus by His name but instead referred to Him as "this man." In the Hebrew language, the name *Jesus* literally means "God saves." The Pharisees didn't want to acknowledge Jesus as Savior, and they certainly didn't want to say "*God saves* is a sinner."

The man born blind but now seeing had nothing helpful to offer concerning whether Jesus was a sinner: "Whether he is a sinner or not, I don't know. One thing I do know. I was blind but now I see!" (John 9:25 NIV).

Obviously this man didn't know everything about

Jesus. But he didn't miss out on Jesus' name or on the miracle He had done. Earlier, when the man came before the Pharisees for the first time, he referred to Him simply as "the man they call Jesus." Later, he called Him "a prophet" (John 9:17). Now he couldn't even tell the Pharisees for sure whether Jesus was a righteous man. All he knew was that Jesus had given him a gift greater than any he could have imagined.

But as this man continued talking to the Pharisees, he seems to have come to a realization about the man called Jesus: "Well, here is an amazing thing, that you do not know where He is from, and yet He opened my eyes. . . . Since the beginning of time it has never been heard that anyone opened the eyes of a person born blind" (John 9:30, 32).

His spiritual eyes were now opening, and the man came to a conclusion about the miracle he had experienced himself: If Jesus had not been from God, then there was no way He could have done what He did for Him (verse 33).

The Pharisees were none too pleased at hearing this truthful observation, and they responded indignantly: "You were born entirely in sins, and you are teaching us?" they snarled at him (verse 34).

That's exactly what he had done. Standing before these pious, self-righteous religious leaders, this man tried to tell them a truth that they were too spiritually blind to see—that by doing such an amazing miracle, Jesus had proved He was from God.

Then, as the Pharisees lost patience with the now-seeing man and threw him out of their presence, something more happened within him. The physical light Jesus had given him when He made his eyes functional became a beam of spiritual light shining into his world.

FROM "KNOWING ABOUT" TO KNOWING HIM

Once again, this now-seeing man met with Jesus personally. This time, Jesus sought him out and finished what He had started when He gave him physical sight. The man was convinced that Jesus was from God, that at the very least He was a prophet. If He wasn't the Messiah, then He knew who was.

"Do you believe in the Son of Man?" Jesus asked him.

"Who is He, Lord, that I may believe in Him?" he asked.

"You have both seen Him, and He is the one who is talking with you," Jesus told him.

The man born blind but now miraculously seeing responded the same way any of us would when Jesus shines His light on us. He not only believed in Jesus, he trusted Him personally and worshiped Him as the Son of God (John 9:35–38). He went from knowing *about* Jesus to knowing Him personally.

What happened to this man is what happens to those of us who have come to know Jesus Christ personally. Like him, we all start out in darkness, but when we acknowledge who Jesus is, when we confess that He is the Son of God and has the power to do miracles in our lives, we are moved from our own darkness and into His light.

When Jesus moves us into a place where we can see His light, then we will never fail to recognize the miraculous movement of God in our lives and in the lives of others.

CONSIDER THIS

Many mature Christians wrestle with the dryness that can come from knowing much *about* Jesus— without the intimacy of truly knowing Him. How can we counteract that tendency?

DIGGING DEEPER

Read about Jesus' various miracles in the Gospels. How did the recipients of those miracles respond, and what can we learn from them?

1. Guido Kuwas, *Global Revival News,* 17 December 2001.

2. Margarita Martinez, "Courtesy Call That Saved a Dying Climber on the Andes," *SundayHerald.com,* 30 June 2002.

CHAPTER SEVEN

PRAISE IN ALL THINGS

There are no miracles for those that have no faith in them.

■ FRENCH PROVERB

"WILL" (NOT HIS REAL NAME) is a good friend of mine who needed a miracle.

I had the privilege of ordaining Will into the ministry, and he had served for several years as the minister of music in the first church I served out of seminary. Will and I became close friends, so close that we were more like brothers.

One day not long ago, I was preparing to preach at a pastor's conference in Jacksonville, Florida, when Will called me and gave me some terrible news. This godly, gifted man with a lovely wife, two fine sons, and a bright future in ministry had cancer, and the doctors gave him little hope of recovery.

Will was devastated at the news. So was I. As we talked, we shared our feelings, cried together, and prayed together that God would do a miracle in Will's body. We prayed He would reach down, touch Will's heart and give him peace.

One ray of hope remained in Will's situation: a small window of time for the doctors to treat him and give him at least a chance to survive. That meant going in for surgery almost immediately and beginning treatment right after the operation.

Within a few days of his call, Will went in for surgery, which his doctors pronounced a success. But Will was not out of the woods yet. He had to begin various treatments that the doctors hoped would kill the rest of the cancer cells.

Miraculously, the surgery and treatment worked. Will's cancer went into remission, and he began his recovery. Within a short time, Will received the wonderful news that his body was cancer free.

Will couldn't say enough about how grateful he was for his recovery. His words and his countenance both spoke of praises to the God he was sure had His healing hand in his recovery. When I talked to Will, we rejoiced together at what we knew was a miracle directly from the hand of God.

But that was not the last trial Will would face as a result of his cancer.

Several months after Will had received the news that his body was free of cancer, he called me again. When I heard his voice, I knew something was terribly wrong. As he greeted me over the phone, his voice sounded grim and hopeless, even more so than when he called me to tell me of his cancer. Immediately, I wondered if the cancer had reappeared.

"Well, son, are you OK physically?" I asked him.

"Physically, God has just moved wonderfully in my life," Will said. "I'm doing fine in that area."

"Then what's wrong?" I asked.

My dear friend fought back tears as he told me that while he was away from work undergoing treatment for the cancer, someone he had hired had gone behind his back and undermined him and undercut him at work, hoping to take over his position.

This man's plan worked perfectly, and now my friend was facing the loss of his job. He didn't know what to do. He asked me if there was anything I could offer to help him through this difficult time.

"Pastor," he said, his voice shaking with pain, "I can take the cancer better than I can take the betrayal."

It was one thing for Will to be hit with a faceless, impartial enemy such as cancer. But it was quite another for him to face the betrayal of someone he believed was a friend and partner in ministry. His heart was broken, and so was mine as I listened to his story.

Will was overwhelmed and under attack on different fronts in his life, and he needed another miracle.

Maybe you've been in that place. Maybe you're there right now. You feel as if you are under attack from different directions and by different enemies. Now, you're overwhelmed and don't know what to do.

How can I overcome? you ask yourself. *How can I get through this storm? What must I do to see a miracle in all of this?*

A king we don't know much about gives us some clues.

ONE WISE LEADER

Jehoshaphat was the fourth king of the Old Testament-era kingdom of Judah. He was the son of and successor to Asa and ruled from 873–849 B.C. The Bible records how Jehoshaphat loved God and wanted more than anything to see the people in his kingdom turn to their God with all their hearts, just as he had.

Shortly after ascending to the throne, Jehoshaphat took two wise steps to strengthen the kingdom of Judah, reinforcing its military and cleansing the land of idolatry. Jehoshaphat knew that many dangerous enemies surrounded his kingdom, so he wanted to make sure Judah was safe from outside invasions. He set up defensive positions around the cities and appointed strong military leaders to lead the troops, with many more garrisons stationed throughout the kingdom (see 2 Chronicles 17:1–2).

Once he had realized his goal of fortifying his kingdom against its enemies, Jehoshaphat took the stronger and even more important step of tending the spiritual condition of his people. The king wanted to remove from his land any hint of idolatry. So in the third year of his reign, he sent out his priests and Levites to teach the Word of God in the cities and encourage the people to turn from any kind of idolatry or pagan worship (see 2 Chronicles 17:7–9).

The result of all Jehoshaphat's work was a spiritual revival in the land of Judah, as well as a time of peace and prosperity. The Bible tells us of a "ripple effect" in which the surrounding kingdoms feared Judah's God and therefore wouldn't dare move against her. In fact, many of those surrounding kingdoms paid tribute to Jehoshaphat and to his successes by bringing the kingdom huge gifts of precious metal and livestock.

Jehoshaphat and his kingdom were flying high for a time. He had in effect defeated his enemies—for the time being—without drawing one sword, and had also presided over a great spiritual revival.

But that would not continue without a huge mistake on Jehoshaphat's part, a mistake that cost him dearly militarily and politically. Yet his mistake can teach us something about the alliances we seek.

MAKING A WRONG ALLIANCE

For reasons most don't fully understand, Jehoshaphat entered into a disastrous alliance with the wicked King Ahab of Israel. On the surface, that might appear to be a good thing. After all, under the rule of King Rehoboam, who was son of and successor to Solomon, the kingdom of Israel had been split, with ten of the twelve tribes withdrawing from his rule to form the Northern Kingdom, or Israel, and the other two forming the Southern Kingdom, or Judah. After that, the two kingdoms had been at odds with one another.

What could be wrong with reuniting—if only for the sake of a military alliance—the two kingdoms that once made up the great empire once known simply as "Israel?"

The problem was with King Ahab himself. He not

only tolerated pagan worship in the Northern Kingdom, but he was married to Jezebel, who as Queen of
Israel had erected idols throughout the land honoring
the false gods.

Jehoshaphat had followed in the footsteps of his
father Asa, who as King of Judah had gone so far as to
drive idol worshippers, including his own grandmother,
Maachah, out of his kingdom. Unfortunately, however, he also followed in his father's footsteps when it
came to forming wrong alliances.

For thirty-six years of his reign, Asa was a great
king who made wise decisions for his kingdom. But in
the face of a military threat from outside the kingdom, instead of turning to God for protection, Asa
panicked and made an alliance with Ben-Hadad, king
of Syria. Politically and militarily, it looked like a
great move. But Asa had done something he'd been
warned against: making alliances with those who
opposed his God.

Asa had lived a blameless life before his God, but
now he had formed a relationship with a man who
had no respect for the Lord or for His Word. God was
not pleased, and He sent a prophet named Hanani
to confront Asa. Hanani pulled no punches when he
told Asa, "You have acted foolishly in this. Indeed,
from now on you will surely have wars" (2 Chronicles
16:9).

Now, Jehoshaphat had made exactly the same
mistake his father had made. He had made an alliance
with, as R.G. Lee, the great twentieth-century Baptist
pastor, called him, "the toad that squatted on the

throne of Israel." And to make matters worse, he created a "family tie" with Ahab when he allowed his son Jehoram to marry Ahab's daughter, Athaliah, making the wicked Jezebel Jehoram's mother-in-law.

Together, the newly aligned kingdoms of Judah and Israel entered into battle against a military power called Ramoth-gilead. It was in this bloody battle that Ahab was killed and the armies of Israel and Judah were defeated.

With his army defeated and his ally dead, Jehoshaphat returned to the safety of his home in Jerusalem. But he wouldn't find peace. Not just yet. That could only come after God, speaking through the prophet Jehu—the son of Hanani, the same Hanani who had scolded Jehoshaphat's father over his ungodly military alliance—confronted the king about his own wrong choice of allies.

"Should you help the wicked and love those who hate the LORD and so bring wrath on yourself from the LORD?" Jehu asked him (2 Chronicles 19:2). But there was good news. Jehu saw Jehoshaphat's heart, and he knew that the man had a heart set on following God.

With those ungodly alliances behind him, Jehoshaphat strengthened his alliance with his God. He continued working to bring the people of Judah back to God and to cleanse the land of any kind of pagan influence.

The timing couldn't have been better.

THE *ONE* RIGHT ALLIANCE

Jehoshaphat had received the news, and it wasn't good. A huge army of men—Moabites, Ammonites, and others—was headed Judah's way.

This army was well trained and armed to the teeth. Maybe this army's commanders thought that Judah's forces would be weakened after the battle with Ramoth-gilead. Maybe they knew about the riches Judah had acquired under the kingship of Jehoshaphat and wanted to take them. The leaders of Judah might not have known this military force's goals, but they knew their intentions.

They meant to attack, and they meant to do it sooner rather than later.

Jehoshaphat had seen the ravages of war up close, and he knew what an attack by an army this size would mean to his kingdom. He knew that countless people—men, women, and children—would die should his kingdom fall. He was afraid.

What was this godly but flawed king to do? Would he turn to a military or diplomatic solution? Would he try to form another alliance with an outside kingdom, hoping it would come to help defend him and his people?

No, he wouldn't do any of those things.

Jehoshaphat had strengthened his alliance with the One who had promised to be with him, the One who had blessed and strengthened his kingdom in the first place. When Jehoshaphat's people needed a miracle just to survive what was headed their way, he did the one thing He knew would save his kingdom: He turned to God. He turned to the only One who could save him and his people at the moment they were overwhelmed and under attack.

Jehoshaphat had come to understand something we ourselves need to understand: When are overwhelmed and under attack, when we are faced with storms and trials, and when we need a miracle to face what is before us, it is vitally important that we make the right alliances.

Our human tendency is to make the wrong kinds of alliances. We grab hold of anything or anyone we think we can depend on. We make alliances with our friends, with people who don't truly care about us, with our own talents and skills, with our education, with our wealth. Then, when we are faced with a crisis it will take a miracle to get us through, those alliances oftentimes fail us.

We can make all kinds of alliances, but there is only One we can trust absolutely to be there for us when we need a miracle. We can't put our absolute trust in any human or institution or in any of our own resources, but we can put that trust in the Lord Jesus Christ.

Rely on anyone but Christ, and you are sure to be discouraged and disappointed when the time comes that you need something more than a break in life or a helping hand. People *may* do what they can to help you out in times of crisis, but our God will go much further than that and actually reach down and carry us through our trials and storms.

The story of Jehoshaphat, this relatively obscure king of Judah who lived nearly twenty-eight centuries ago, teaches us how important it is to God that we make the right alliances.

But Jehoshaphat's story teaches us another lesson: When we need a miracle, it may be that God is calling us to specific action.

THE PRAYER OF . . . JEHOSHAPHAT?

Word had gotten out that a military force very likely larger than anything the kings, leaders, and people of Judah had ever heard of was set to attack. Jehoshaphat's army, badly outnumbered and weakened by an earlier war, faced what appeared to be certain and overwhelming defeat.

Jehoshaphat knew what was coming, and he not only turned to God himself, he also called his people to do the same. He proclaimed a fast throughout all of Judah, and called his people to gather and take action.

In the scene described early in 2 Chronicles 20, there is no "pep talk" on the part of the King of Judah, no final words to his troops before they head out to war. Instead, there is an entire kingdom gathered before their king, who prepares them and himself by doing one thing: praying and falling down in worship before the Lord!

A few years ago, a small book came seemingly out of nowhere to take not just Christian book publishing but the book publishing industry in general by storm. Bruce Wilkinson's *The Prayer of Jabez*, which was based on a short prayer uttered by a nearly unknown Bible character and recorded in the fourth chapter of 1 Chronicles, sold millions of copies worldwide.

The premise of *The Prayer of Jabez* is that when we use Jabez's life-changing prayer as a model in our own prayers, God will bless us and "enlarge our kingdoms."

But in 2 Chronicles 20, we see a model prayer as powerful and life-changing as just about any recorded in the Bible. With men, women, and children of all ages gathered before him, Jehoshaphat utters a prayer that draws heavily on powerful prayers by his ancestors, Kings David and Solomon, as well as those of Moses.

Jehoshaphat's prayer demonstrates five key aspects of effective prayer, all of which we should remember when we need a miracle.

1. *Recognition.* Jehoshaphat's powerful prayer begins with a simple recognition, not of his kingdom's condition or the threat facing it, but of the person, character, and attributes of his God. The prayer is very much like that of King David, Jehoshaphat's great, great, great grandfather as recorded in 1 Chronicles 29, when he prayed after the people began to give to the building of the temple.

Jehoshaphat's powerful prayer starts with two simple questions:

- "Art Thou not God in the heavens?"
- "Art Thou not ruler over all the kingdoms of the nations?"

These are what we could call rhetorical questions, meaning that the answer is included in the question itself. In other words, Jehoshaphat doesn't ask these questions in order to receive an answer; he already knows the answer. He isn't really asking God these questions; rather, he's offering humble recognition to the God he knows is over everything and all-powerful in the face of anything his enemies throw his way.

Jehoshaphat needed a miracle, and as he sought God and asked for that miracle, he started by recognizing some things about God Himself.

Does this mean that God needs to be reminded that He is above all and all-powerful? Not at all! Rather, it means that when we are seeking God and asking Him to perform a miracle on our behalf, *we need to recognize who He is and what He can do.*

I've had an ongoing debate with my youngest son about whether prayer changes God's mind about what He's going to do. In other words, does prayer really *change things?* I believe I could write a whole book on that subject, but for now I want to tell you one thing I know for sure about prayer: It *changes us!* When we make the kinds of recognitions about our God Jehoshaphat made, it changes our hearts and minds. Courage replaces fear. Peace replaces anxiety. Faith replaces doubt.

When life has us feeling overwhelmed, under attack, and out of hope, we need to stop and prayerfully acknowledge God's power over every situation we face. That is the beginning of seeing God do miracles for us. But it is just the beginning!

2. Recollection. Once Jehoshaphat had made a personal recognition of God's greatness, he asked yet another rhetorical question: "Did You not, O our God, drive out the inhabitants of this land before Your people Israel, and give it to the descendants of Abraham Your friend forever?" (2 Chronicles 20:7).

Jehoshaphat is doing exactly what Moses did when he cautioned the people of Israel not to forget the things God had done for them. In Deuteronomy 8, we can read of Moses' warnings to the Hebrews not to forget those things:

- "And you shall remember . . ." (8:2)
- "Beware lest you forget . . ." (8:11)
- "But you shall remember . . ." (8:18)
- "If you ever forget . . ." (8:19)

In his prayer, Jehoshaphat commemorates how God had cared for His people in the past. He remembers how God had prepared the way for the Israelites to settle in the Promised Land and how He stayed with them and cared for them.

When we are facing life storms and trials and needing a miracle, we need faith, and part of what strengthens that faith is remembering how God has blessed us in the past. When we remember those things, we can rest assured, knowing that if God moved for us before—and He has—then He will surely move again.

3. Recitation. Standing approximately where his great, great grandfather King Solomon stood when he prayed—at the front of the temple—Jehoshaphat prays a prayer of deliverance to his God:

"They lived in it, and have built You a sanctuary there for Your name, saying, 'Should evil come upon us, the sword or judgment, or pestilence, or famine, we will stand before this house and before You (for

Your name is in this house) and cry to You in our distress, and You will hear and deliver us'" (2 Chronicles 20:8–9).

This part of Jehoshaphat's prayer sounds very similar to Solomon's prayer in 2 Chronicles 6: "that Your eye may be open toward this house day and night, toward the place of which You have said that You would put Your name there, to listen to the prayer which Your servant shall pray toward this place. And listen to the supplications of Your people Israel, when they pray toward this place; hear from Your dwelling place, from heaven; hear and forgive" (6:20–21, NASB).

Jehoshaphat, then, was reciting the revealed Word of God as he prayed for deliverance. And when we are looking for deliverance—when we are looking for a miracle—we need to do the same.

Jehoshaphat recited something we in need of a miracle need to recite for ourselves: "We will stand before you, God, and cry to you in times of trouble, and you will hear us and deliver us!"

We can always rest in the certainty that God will agree with His own words. In other words, if it's in the Bible, you can bank on it! So when you are overwhelmed with life, at the end of your rope, and needing a miracle, recite the promises of God and recite them in prayer. And do it *knowing* that He'll hear you!

4. *Confession.* Jehoshaphat sets the stage for a great miracle of God when he makes this confession: "We are powerless . . . nor do we know what to do" (2 Chronicles 20:12).

Just moments before, Jehoshaphat confessed that the kingdom of Judah was in a situation that they could do nothing about. All of these outside kingdoms, all of them nations God kept the Hebrews from invading as they made their way through the wilderness to the Promised land, are now returning their good with evil.

This praying king confessed to God what just about everyone at the scene knew, namely that there was no way the military of Judah could stand before the thousands of soldiers who were poised for attack, that they were sunk unless the Lord intervened and performed a miracle.

Finally, Jehoshaphat makes the second part of his confession, the part so key for one looking for God to perform a miracle: "Our eyes are on Thee" (verse 12).

Sometimes that is a difficult confession. It means admitting to God and to others that we are powerless, weak, and helpless, that unless we keep our eyes on Jesus we're sunk. It means we will take our eyes off our trials and storms and keep them on the Lord. But this is one confession we need to make when we want God to perform a miracle. It's one we will be glad we made!

Jehoshaphat made this very confession, and it unified the people of Judah before God (2 Chronicles 20:13). Each man, woman and child of the kingdom stood before their Lord, confessing as one that they were powerless and had nowhere to turn but to Him.

God responded to them. Right there on the spot—not the next day or next week—God answered the people's prayers.

A RESPONSE FROM ABOVE

When God responded to His people's confessions and cries for help, He did it in a way many of us aren't used to seeing: immediately.

Many of us have a hard time believing that God can or will work fast in a crisis situation. But He can, and this time He did. While God doesn't always respond to our cries for help immediately, He always answers at just the right time. In this case, God knew the situation better than the people did, and He knew that answering tomorrow or next week was not an option. His people were going to be attacked within the next day or two, so He took swift action.

Jehoshaphat had no sooner finished praying when the Holy Spirit moved and spoke through a Levite by the name of Jahaziel. The first word out of Jahaziel's mouth is one of both instruction and comfort to the people: *"Listen!"*

God had heard His people's cry for help, now He wanted them to hear Him.

"Listen, all Judah and the inhabitants of Jerusalem and King Jehoshaphat: thus says the Lord to you, 'Do not fear or be dismayed because of this great multitude, for the battle is not yours but God's'" (2 Chronicles 20:15).

Everybody was called to listen, to slow down and take their eyes off what was before them, and hear very clearly what God had to say. God wanted the people to know that He understood that they were frightened and confused, that they didn't know what to do, that they were absolutely powerless in the face of this very real threat.

But the Lord also wanted His people to know that He was taking away any cause for fear. Yes, He was sending them out to the enemy—He even told them specifically where and when they would find this massive army (verse 16).

God didn't instruct the people to cut and run or to surrender. Rather, He told them to stand up to the enemy. But He also let them know that the battle was already won. Why? Because it was His battle, not theirs.

Those words had to be an overwhelming comfort to Jehoshaphat and to his people. And they should be a comfort to us too. When we need a miracle, when only action on the part of God Himself can rescue us, we need to remember that our God has never lost any kind of battle with any kind of enemy.

This doesn't mean that we, ourselves, won't face some very real enemies, and great difficulties, in life. What it means is we can have an absolute confidence that when we put our trust in God, when we confess to Him that we are powerless and don't know what to do, we can be assured that ultimately our Lord gives us victory.

While writing this chapter I have just preached the funeral of a wonderful forty-two-year-old husband and father. I remember well the beautiful May Sunday morning when Chuck and his sweet wife and eight-year-old daughter joined First Dallas. It was later that week that Chuck was diagnosed with cancer. He did not live quite a year. His last time in worship was Easter Sunday morning when we baptized his daughter. He died several weeks later.

His wife, Laura, shared with me that it was the Sunday after they discovered that the treatments were not working, and the doctors told him there was nothing else they could do, that they were in church and the congregation was singing "It Is Well With My Soul." She said Chuck leaned on the pew in front of him, trying to hold himself up, as he sang out:

> When peace, like a river, attendeth my way,
>
> When sorrows like sea billows roll;
>
> Whatever my lot, Thou hast taught me to say,
>
> It is well, it is well, with my soul.

There was the sense of absolute confidence that even in death God was victorious.

Those many centuries ago, right on the spot, God spoke to the people of Judah, telling them that there would indeed be a battle, but not to be afraid or worried.

Then He instructed the people to get up the next morning and face the enemy.

But the weapons of this battle weren't going to be swords, spears, arrows, or slings. Rather, they were simple words: words of praise spoken and sung to their Lord.

PRAISE AS A WEAPON

When Jehoshaphat and the people of Judah heard the comforting words from the Lord, they could do

nothing else but worship Him. The king fell on his
face and worshiped God, while the choir got up to
sing songs of praise.

But that was not the end of the celebration.

Early the next morning, the army of Judah headed
out to meet its foe. But leading the mission wasn't
the military scouts or the best fighting men the kingdom had to offer. Instead, it was the choir.

"Give thanks to the Lord, for His lovingkindness is
everlasting," (verse 21) they sang out loudly as they
marched toward the battlefield.

As He had promised, before the people of Judah
had even seen the enemy, God had gone before them
and finished the battle. The armies of Ammon, Moab,
and Mount Seir had turned on one another, and by
the time the army of Judah arrived on the scene, not
one of the enemy soldiers was left standing.

God had in fact turned the enemy on itself, leaving
the army of Judah with nothing to do but haul away
the spoils.

And all of that after doing nothing but singing
praises to their God!

Jehoshaphat gave us a beautiful example of what
we should do when we are looking for a miracle. First,
he formed an alliance with His God. Then, when he
was faced with disaster, he was able to turn to the
Lord and seek help. And before God had reached
down and performed that miracle, Jehoshaphat led
his people in words and songs of praise for Him.

When we are looking for a miracle, we need to
remember that that there is great power in speaking

simple words of praise to our Lord.

When we are in the midst of a financial disaster, we should praise His name.

When we are going through a family crisis, we should praise His name.

When we are facing a possibly life-threatening illness, we should praise His name.

In all things, we should praise His name.

Indeed, praise is a powerful weapon for spiritual warfare as well as for bringing about the miraculous.

I have discovered that praise changes the entire complexion and mood of the people of God. I believe that is because, as David the psalmist wrote, that the Lord inhabits the praise of His people (see Psalm 22:3).

Dr. Mark Corts, longtime pastor of Calvary Baptist Church in Winston-Salem, North Carolina, once told me that a preacher should never go into a critical business meeting without leading the people of God in a time of praise.

D. L. Moody, preaching out of 2 Chronicles 5, which tells us about the dedication of God's temple, stated that Solomon prevailed much in prayer, "but it was the voice of praise which brought down the glory that filled the house."

Paul Billheimer—author of such books as *Destined for the Throne, Destined to Overcome,* and *Destined for the Cross*—once wrote: "Satan is allergic to praise, so where there is massive triumphant praise, Satan is paralyzed, bound, and banished."

Mary Slosser, a missionary to China, once said: "I sing the Doxology and dismiss the devil."

Amy Carmichael, the Irish-born missionary of the early 1900s, said: "I believe truly that Satan cannot endure it and so slips out of the room—more or less—when there is true song."

William Law, in his spiritual classic *A Serious Call to a Devout and Holy Life,* wrote: "There is nothing that so clears the way for your prayers, nothing that so disperses dullness of heart, nothing that so purifies the soul from poor and little passions, nothing that so opens heaven, or carries your heart so near it, as these songs of praise."

On January 8, 1956, Jim Elliot and four other young missionaries to Ecuador approached the jungle's edge, where the Auca Indians lived. All five of these people were soon to die as martyrs at the hands of the natives. And their last act before they entered the natives' village, according to Elisabeth Elliot, was to sing a hymn of praise together:

> *We go in faith, our own great weakness feeling,*
>
> *And needing more each day Thy grace to know.*
>
> *Yes from our hearts a song of Triumph pealing,*
>
> *We rest in Thee, and in thy name we go.*

These are all outstanding examples of what can happen when we open our mouths and hearts to praise our God. When we follow them, we will see that it's time for a miracle!

CONSIDER THIS

If you already keep a journal, begin writing down some praises to God. If you don't keep a journal, consider writing some praises anyway. Be specific, focusing on both who He is and what He has done for you.

DIGGING DEEPER

We can tend to skip over the detailed chronicles of Israel's history, believing it doesn't apply to our concerns today. Beginning with 1 and 2 Chronicles, study some of these historical texts and ponder their relevance to us today.

Since 1894, Moody Publishers has been dedicated to equip and motivate people to advance the cause of Christ by publishing evangelical Christian literature and other media for all ages, around the world. Because we are a ministry of the Moody Bible Institute of Chicago, a portion of the proceeds from the sale of this book go to train the next generation of Christian leaders.

If we may serve you in any way in your spiritual journey toward understanding Christ and the Christian life, please contact us at www.moodypublishers.com.

"All Scripture is God-breathed and is useful for teaching, rebuking, correcting and training in righteousness, so that the man of God may be thoroughly equipped for every good work."
—2 TIMOTHY 3:16, 17

MOODY
PUBLISHERS

THE NAME YOU CAN TRUST

THE MIRACLE YOU'VE BEEN SEARCHING FOR TEAM

ACQUIRING EDITOR
Mark Tobey

COPY EDITOR
Allan Sholes

BACK COVER COPY
Michele Straubel

COVER DESIGN
Paetzold Associates

INTERIOR DESIGN
Ragont Design

PRINTING AND BINDING
Quebecor World Book Services

The typeface for the text of this book is
Giovanni